To Joel, as always.

Implementing ISO 14001

Also available from ASQC Quality Press

The ISO 14000 Handbook
Joseph Cascio, editor

What Is ISO 14000? Questions and Answers, Second Edition
Caroline G. Hemenway, editor

Eight-Step Process to Successful ISO 9000 Implementation:
A Quality Management System Approach
Lawrence A. Wilson

The ISO 9000 Auditor's Companion
Kent A. Keeney

After the Quality Audit: Closing the Loop on the Audit Process
J. P. Russell and Terry Regel

To request a complimentary catalog of publications, call 800-248-1946.

Implementing ISO 14001

Marilyn R. Block

ASQC Quality Press
Milwaukee, Wisconsin

Implementing ISO 14001
Marilyn R. Block

Library of Congress Cataloging-in-Publication Data
Block, Marilyn R.
  Implementing ISO 14001 / Marilyn R. Block.
    p. cm.
  Includes bibliographical references and index.
  ISBN 0-87389-357-3 (alk. paper)
  1. ISO 14000 Series Standards. 2. Manufacturers—Environmental
aspects.   I. Title.
TS155.7.B56   1997
658.4'08—dc20   96-27181
                                                              CIP

10 9 8 7 6 5 4 3 2 1

ISBN 0-87389-357-3

Acquisitions Editor: Roger Holloway
Project Editor: Jeanne W. Bohn

ASQC Mission: To facilitate continuous improvement and increase customer satisfaction
by identifying, communicating, and promoting the use of quality principles, concepts, and
technologies; and thereby be recognized throughout the world as the leading authority on,
and champion for, quality.

Attention: Schools and Corporations
ASQC Quality Press books, audiotapes, videotapes, and software are available at
quantity discounts with bulk purchases for business, educational, or instructional use.
For information, please contact ASQC Quality Press at 800-248-1946, or write to
ASQC Quality Press, P.O. Box 3005, Milwaukee, WI 53201-3005.

For a free copy of the ASQC Quality Press Publications Catalog, including ASQC membership information, call 800-248-1946.

Printed in the United States of America

∞ Printed on acid-free paper

Quality Press
611 East Wisconsin Avenue
Milwaukee, Wisconsin 53202

Preface

Recent publication of the ISO 14001 environmental management system (EMS) specification standard has spurred a plethora of books about the ISO 14000 series standards. Most of these provide a general overview of the 17 standards contained under the ISO 14000 umbrella.

Implementing ISO 14001 goes beyond general description to identify the ways in which ISO 14001 can be implemented within the constraints of business strategies, environmental imperatives, and regulatory requirements. It offers an effective guideline that walks an organization's staff through the process of assessing its existing EMS, comparing it to ISO 14001, identifying weak or missing elements, and modifying the EMS to conform to the ISO 14001 requirements. This information will particularly interest

- Midlevel and senior-level environmental managers who are considering or have a mandate to attain conformance to an effective EMS.

- Environmental staff in small and medium-sized companies that are likely to be affected by ISO 14001 as a function of their supplier status to multinational corporations.

- Auditors, trainers, consultants, and others who do not have hands-on experience with ISO 14001, but are encountering growing interest among their company clients.

The book is organized into three sections that enable the reader to move directly to issues of particular interest.

Section I, Understanding ISO 14000, is written for those who are not familiar with the ISO standards-setting process in general and ISO 14000 in particular. Chapter 1, Background and Development of ISO 14000, delineates the organizational structure and mandate of the technical committee charged with creating the ISO 14000 series standards and describes the process by which it pursued that task. Chapter 2, Standards in the ISO 14000 Series, briefly describes the 17 standards that comprise ISO 14000. Chapter 3, National and Regional Concerns, examines the importance of EMS standards throughout Europe and in Mexico, two regions of paramount importance to numerous U.S. companies. National adoption of the standard in Japan and the United States is also discussed.

Section II, Executing ISO 14001, is designed to assist those who are familiar with ISO 14001 and seek to better understand whether and how it might be implemented within their own organizations. Chapter 4, Why to Implement ISO 14001, describes the uses of ISO 14001. Chapter 5, Understanding ISO 14001, presents the 17 required elements and discusses what companies are expected to accomplish. Chapter 6, Assessing an Existing Environmental Management System, focuses on the first step in determining what will be involved in the successful implementation of ISO 14001—gap analysis—and describes the experience of the H.B. Fuller Company in conducting a gap analysis of its EMS. Chapter 7, Integrating ISO 14001 with an Existing Environmental Management System, presents the experiences of and lessons learned by United Technologies Corporation, a diversified multinational corporation committed to integrating ISO 14001 with its existing EMS.

Section III, Comparing ISO 14001 to Other Standards, is written for those who are familiar with ISO 9000, other EMS standards, or industry codes of practice. This section illustrates similarities and differences between ISO 14001 and a number of other standards.

ISO 14001 is generating a high level of interest as the EMS framework of choice, even in companies that do not plan to pursue formal registration, for several reasons.

- It contains core elements that have garnered international consensus.

- It allows multinational companies to implement a single EMS in varied locations, thereby eliminating the need to conform to numerous national standards.

- It can be integrated with ISO 9001 and ISO 9002.

- It fulfills specific customer requirements.

Implementing ISO 14001 begins where most other books stop. It provides practical guidance in the areas of strategic planning, environmental affairs, quality, and government affairs for managers who must determine whether ISO 14001 is the right thing to do and how to initiate a process that capitalizes on existing strengths and successes.

Note About ISO 14001

All references in this book to ISO 14001 pertain to ISO 14001, *Environmental management systems—Specification with guidance for use.* Interpretation of various elements of ISO 14001 is based on the author's participation as a member of the American National Standards Institute's U.S. Technical Advisory Group to ISO/TC 207 and as one of the U.S. delegates to ISO/TC 207's Subcommittee 1— Environmental Management Systems, which developed ISO 14001 and the accompanying guideline ISO 14004.

Acknowledgments

The route to this book began in 1988 when Tom Ingersoll and Gardiner Shaw shared their preliminary thinking about applying total quality management (TQM) principles to the management of environmental issues. The journey was assisted by a number of individuals; most notably Bill Leslie, who has forgotten more about TQM than most people ever learn, and Susan Vogt, whose enthusiasm encouraged me to move into the world of international standards development.

Establishment of ISO Technical Committee 207 provided a significant milestone that was enhanced by the opportunity I had to work with and learn from Joel Charm, whose grace under pressure was inspirational; Phil Marcus, who taught me much about international negotiation; and the many members of the U.S. Technical Advisory Group, especially Chris Bell, Fred McCarty, Connie Ritzert, Eldon Rucker, Amy Schaffer, and Richard Wells, who generously provided the chapter 3 portion on ISO 14001 in Mexico.

I wish to sincerely thank the H.B. Fuller Company and United Technologies Corporation for their willingness to provide access to internal resources and information concerning their ISO 14001 experiences.

Finally, I extend heartfelt appreciation to Camp Matens, without whose support my active participation as a delegate to ISO/TC 207 and, therefore, this book, would not have been possible.

Section I

Understanding ISO 14000

Chapter 1

Background and Development of ISO 14000

Background

The International Organization for Standardization, ISO, was established in 1947 to expand trade, improve quality, increase productivity, and reduce costs of goods and services through worldwide agreement on international standards. During its 50-year history, ISO has published more than 3000 technical and nontechnical standards in all fields except electrotechnical. Electrotechnical standards fall under the purview of the International Electrotechnical Commission (IEC), established in 1906.

The genesis of ISO 14000 occurred in 1990 with the creation of the Business Charter for Sustainable Development (BCSD), an organization of 50 business leaders with an interest in environment and development issues. The premise underlying its work is that economic development can only happen in a healthy environment.

In mid-1991, partially as a result of the work of the BCSD and partially in anticipation of the 1992 United Nations Conference on Environment and Development in Rio de Janeiro, ISO created the Strategic Advisory Group on the Environment (SAGE) to assess the need for an international standard on environmental management. In the spring of 1993, SAGE recommended that ISO develop what has become known as ISO 14000. SAGE, established as an ad hoc committee, was replaced by ISO Technical Committee (TC) 207, which was mandated to standardize worldwide environmental management systems and tools in the following areas.

- Environmental management systems (EMS)

- Environmental auditing

- Environmental labeling

3

- Environmental performance evaluation (EPE)
- Life cycle assessment (LCA)
- Terms and definitions
- Environmental aspects in product standards (EAPS)

Although national and regional environmental management standards have proliferated in the past few years, the cultural blinders that accompany such efforts often result in unintended technical barriers to international trade. ISO 14000, which is being developed by delegations from nearly 50 countries, is intended to create tools and systems that will improve corporate environmental performance and safeguard companies against negative impacts on trade and commerce.

TC 207 Structure

In an effort to break its business plan into manageable chunks, TC 207 employs a multitiered structure. At the top of the organizational pyramid is TC 207, which oversees the general standards development process and related administrative functions. The secretariat for TC 207 resides in Canada.

The second tier of the TC 207 organizational pyramid consists of subcommittees (SCs). SCs are responsible for the development of standards within a defined area (see Figure 1.1). The EAPS standard was

SC number	Area of responsibility	Secretariat
SC1	Environmental management systems	United Kingdom
SC2	Environmental auditing	The Netherlands
SC3	Environmental labeling	Australia
SC4	Environmental performance evaluation	United States
SC5	Life cycle assessment	Germany
SC6	Terms and definitions	Norway
WG	Environmental aspects in product standards	Germany

Figure 1.1. TC 207 subcommittee secretariats.

assigned to a work group (WG) rather than an SC; however, the WG chair reports to the chair of TC 207 rather than to an SC chair.

The third tier of the TC 207 organization chart is composed of work groups (WGs). These WGs can be thought of as drafting committees. With few exceptions, each WG is creating an individual standard within its SC's assigned area. The exceptions are found in SC4 and SC5, where two WGs are working on single documents.

The TC 207 Process

ISO requires a consensus process in the development of standards, from initial draft to final publication.

• A WG creates a working draft (WD) standard. WG members share the draft within their own countries by whatever mechanism has been established. ("U.S. Technical Advisory Group," starting on page 7, describes the mechanism in the United States.)

• The WD is revised to reflect the comments of participating delegations. WG members then share the revised WD within their own countries. This process is repeated until the WG achieves consensus on its WD.

• The WD is presented to the SC for acceptance as a committee draft (CD). Although not required by ISO, SCs have opted to distribute CDs to SC members for comment. Written comments submitted by national delegations are reviewed by the responsible WG and integrated where consensus is achieved.

• The CD is distributed as a *CD for ballot* to all SC members who are asked to respond to one of four options. The four options are to

—Approve the CD, as written, as a draft international standard (DIS).

—Approve the CD as a DIS with comments.

—Disapprove the CD as a DIS. Delegations that select this option must submit a written explanation of the reasons for disapproval with their ballots.

—Abstain.

Participating delegations have three months to return their ballots. If two-thirds of the returned ballots indicate approval, with or without comments, the CD is ready for elevation to a DIS.

• Comments submitted with ballots are reviewed by the appropriate WG, and those comments for which consensus is achieved are integrated into the DIS. At this point, resolutions are made at SC and TC meetings to elevate the document to DIS status. If the resolutions are passed, the document is designated a DIS.

• The DIS is distributed to TC 207 members, who have six months to return a ballot that approves or disapproves the DIS as an ISO standard. At this stage, comments are expected to be editorial in nature. The DIS must be approved by two-thirds of the returned ballots and cannot be disapproved by more than 25 percent of ISO members.

• If the DIS is approved, the SC secretariat incorporates all appropriate editorial changes. A final ballot is distributed to ISO members, who have two months to approve or disapprove the revised DIS (referred to as a *final* or FDIS) as an ISO standard. No comments are accepted during this final two-month ballot stage.

All ISO standards must be reaffirmed, revised, or withdrawn periodically, usually every five years. A liaison group of representatives from TC 207 and TC 176, the ISO technical committee that developed the ISO 9000 quality management system standards, is considering whether ISO 14001 will be readdressed just three years after publication, in 1999, to synchronize its revision schedule with that of the ISO 9000 series standards.

TC 207 Participants

Membership in ISO is open to national standards-setting organizations. Approximately 110 countries are ISO members, including the United States. The United States is represented by the American National Standards Institute (ANSI).

ISO members are free to join any TC in which they are interested. Forty-three countries have taken an active role in the development of ISO 14000 (see Figure 1.2).

Argentina	Indonesia	South Africa
Australia	Ireland	South Korea
Belgium	Israel	Spain
Brazil	Italy	Sweden
Canada	Jamaica	Switzerland
Chile	Japan	Tanzania
China	Malaysia	Thailand
Colombia	Mexico	Turkey
Cuba	Netherlands	Trinidad
Czechoslovakia	New Zealand	United Kingdom
Denmark	North Korea	United States
Finland	Norway	Uruguay
France	Philippines	Venezuela
Germany	Russian Federation	
India	Singapore	

Figure 1.2. Participating TC 207 members.

U.S. Technical Advisory Group

To ensure that those who will be affected by ISO 14000 had an opportunity to contribute to the review of draft documents and the formation of the U.S. negotiating positions at various international TC, SC, and WG meetings, ANSI created the U.S. Technical Advisory Group (TAG) to TC 207. The TAG is accredited by ANSI to conduct work on international standardization activities pertaining to ISO 14000.

TAG membership is open to companies, organizations, government agencies, and individuals. Of the approximately 575 TAG members, there are 100 FORTUNE 500 companies, 15 industry associations, 7 government agencies including the Environmental Protection Agency (EPA), and 13 special interest organizations such as the Environmental Defense Fund and the National Wildlife Federation. Most of the remaining members are medium-sized and small companies, law firms, and consulting companies.

The TAG's primary responsibility is to develop and transmit to ISO, via ANSI, the U.S. position on activities and ballots of ISO/TC 207. Other TAG functions include the following activities.

- Initiating and approving U.S. proposals for new work items for TC 207 or an SC

- Determining U.S. positions on various documents before TC 207, an SC, or a WG

- Assuring adequate representation at international meetings of TC 207, SCs, and WGs

In order to thoroughly participate in the broad range of SC and WG activities, the TAG established subcommittees—referred to as sub-TAGs to differentiate them from TC 207 SCs—that parallel the TC 207 SC structure. Sub-TAGs review all material developed by their assigned SC, recommend (for TAG approval) the U.S. response, and ensure that U.S. interests are appropriately and adequately represented at international SC and WG meetings.

At ANSI's request, the American Society for Testing and Materials (ASTM) serves as the TAG administrator and is responsible for providing all logistical support. This includes arranging meetings, distributing documents, and generally facilitating the exchange of information among TAG members. ASTM also serves as the administrator for the sub-TAGs on environmental performance evaluation, life cycle assessment, terms and definitions, and environmental aspects in product standards.

Similarly, ASQC serves as the administrator for the sub-TAGs on environmental management systems and environmental auditing. NSF International fulfills the administrator function for the sub-TAG on environmental labeling.

The U.S. TAG was actively involved in all phases of ISO 14001 development. The final standard reflects most of the U.S. TAG positions.

Chapter 2

The Standards in the ISO 14000 Series

As described in chapter 1, ISO/TC 207 is organized into subcommittees that are responsible for the five clusters of standards that comprise the ISO 14000 series—environmental management systems, environmental auditing, environmental labeling, environmental performance evaluation, and life cycle assessment (LCA).

ISO standards are of two types.

1. *Normative* standards specify requirements that must be met and are auditable for certification.

2. *Informative* standards provide guidance only. As such, they are not requirements for certification and, therefore, are not auditable.

ISO 14001, *Environmental management systems—Specification with guidance for use,* is the only normative standard in the ISO 14000 series. All other ISO 14000 series standards are informative and intended to support implementation of the EMS. The standards in the ISO 14000 series are listed in Figure 2.1. Appendix B contains the table of contents for each standard in the ISO 14000 series. It is likely that revisions to those standards in working draft form will result in changes to their respective contents. However, this information is presented to provide the reader with an overview of the issues covered by each standard.

SC1: Environmental Management Systems

It is important to understand that ISO 14001 is an environmental *management* standard; it is not an environmental *performance* standard. Therefore, it focuses on the core elements of an EMS without

Standard number	Title
ISO 14001	*Environmental management systems—Specification with guidance for use*
ISO 14004	*Environmental management systems—General guidelines on principles, systems and supporting techniques*
ISO 14010	*Guidelines for environmental auditing—General principles*
ISO 14011	*Guidelines for environmental auditing—Audit procedures—Auditing of environmental management systems*
ISO 14012	*Guidelines for environmental auditing—Qualification criteria for environmental auditors*
ISO 14020	*General principles for all environmental labels and declarations*
ISO 14021	*Environmental labels and declarations—Self-declaration environmental claims—Terms and definitions*
ISO 14022	*Environmental labels and declarations—Self-declaration environmental claims—Symbols*
ISO 14023	*Environmental labels and declarations—Self-declaration environmental claims—Testing and verification*
ISO 14024	*Environmental labels and declarations—Type I guiding principles and procedures*
ISO 14031	*Environmental management—Environmental performance evaluation guideline*
ISO 14040	*Life cycle assessment—Principles and framework*
ISO 14041	*Life cycle assessment—Inventory analysis*
ISO 14042	*Life cycle assessment—Impact assessment*
ISO 14043	*Life cycle assessment—Interpretation*
ISO 14050	*Terms and Definitions*
ISO 14060	*Guide for the inclusion of environmental aspects in product standards*

Figure 2.1. ISO 14000 environmental management standards.

delineating specific performance targets. ISO 14001 is discussed in detail in chapter 5.

In addition to the EMS specification, SC1 has developed a guidelines standard, ISO 14004, that delineates issues for consideration in implementing an EMS. It also attempts to provide practical help and suggestions for companies that are considering implementing an EMS for the first time. Although intended as a guideline for all organizations, ISO 14004 is likely to be most helpful to those companies that have little or no experience with establishing and implementing an EMS.

SC2: Environmental Auditing

SC2 has developed three environmental audit standards. ISO 14010 delineates seven general principles of environmental auditing that are applicable to any type of environmental audit. Specifically, the standard addresses the following.

1. *Objectives and scope*—Objectives are defined by the client—that is, the organization commissioning the environmental audit. The scope establishes the extent of the audit to meet stated objectives.

2. *Objectivity, independence, and competence*—Audit team members should be free from bias and conflict of interest. They should possess the knowledge, skills, and experience necessary to fulfill audit responsibilities.

3. *Due professional care*—This principle stresses confidentiality of information obtained during the course of an environmental audit and the final report, unless disclosure is approved by the client or required by law.

4. *Systematic procedures*—Environmental audits should be conducted according to documented and well-defined methodologies.

5. *Audit criteria, evidence, and findings*—This principle suggests that the quality of audit evidence should be such that competent environmental auditors, working independently of each other, would reach similar findings.

6. *Reliability of audit findings and conclusions*—The need for environmental auditors to understand that their audits are based on samples of information and, therefore, contain some level of uncertainty is stressed.

7. *Reporting*—Audit findings should be communicated in a written report.

ISO 14011 is intended to establish procedures for planning and performing an EMS audit. It is more detailed than the general principles standard. Two sections are of particular interest.

Section 4, Environmental Management System Audit Objectives, Roles, and Responsibilities states that an EMS audit should have defined objectives and provides five examples of typical EMS audit objectives. It also describes responsibilities and activities of lead auditors, auditors, the audit team, the client, and the auditee (who may or may not be the client).

Section 5, Auditing, focuses on the following areas.

- Initiating the audit, including audit scope and preliminary document review

- Preparing the audit, including audit plan, audit team assignments, and working documents

- Executing the audit, including the opening meeting, collecting evidence, audit findings, and the closing meeting

- Audit reports and records, including audit report preparation, report content, report distribution, and document retention

Auditors who have never conducted an EMS audit will find ISO 14011 of limited value. It focuses on the technical aspects of conducting an audit without articulating how an EMS audit differs from other types of environmental audits. For example, the standard states that sufficient evidence should be collected to be able to determine whether the auditee's EMS conforms to the EMS audit criteria (section 5.3.2). The failure of the standard to describe the kinds of evidence that are appropriate to an EMS audit will leave readers with the feeling that ISO 14011 is little more than another general principles document.

In fact, SC2 has discussed integrating ISO 14010 and 14011 into a single standard at some future date, possibly during the revision process. While this is likely to result in a comprehensive general principles standard, similar to ISO 10011-1, *Guidelines for auditing quality systems*, it will do little to provide guidance for the EMS auditor.

Guidance is found in ISO 14012 on qualification criteria for environmental auditors who might be selected by an organization to conduct different types of environmental audits. This standard provides criteria for auditors and lead auditors. It also applies to internal and external auditors.

SC3: Environmental Labeling

SC3 is developing five standards with the broad objective of reducing the environmental impacts associated with the consumption of products and services. The train of logic employed by the SC members runs on the following track.

- Environmental labels and declarations provide information about the overall environmental character or specific environmental attributes of a product or service.

- Purchasers can use such information if environmental considerations are deemed important in selecting a product or service.

- If environmental labels/declarations influence purchasing decisions, market share will increase.

- Competitors, faced with shrinking market share, will respond by improving the environmental attributes of their products or services in order to make similar environmental claims.

- The environmental burdens associated with the product or service category will be reduced.

A word of explanation is necessary to clarify how SC3 refers to various labeling programs. When SC3 developed its business plan in 1993, it listed the kinds of labeling programs for which standards would be developed: criteria-based certification programs, manufacturer self-declaration claims, and environmental report cards. As an internal shorthand, these were identified as type I, type II, and type III programs, respectively.

ISO 14020 delineates nine principles on which all types of environmental labels and declarations should be based. Environmental labeling that conforms to these principles should result in accurate, verifiable, and relevant communication of information about the environmental aspects of the product or service of interest.

Three standards specifically address self-declaration environmental claims (type II). As defined by SC3, such claims are made without independent third-party certification by manufacturers, importers, distributors, retailers, or others likely to benefit from the claim.

ISO 14021 defines and give rules for the use of specific terms used in environmental claims. It is intended to minimize unwarranted claims, thereby reducing marketplace confusion and enabling purchasers to make informed choices. ISO 14021 addresses the following areas.

- Basic criteria for making claims

- Relevance and verification of environmental claims

- Definition of specific terms and restrictions/qualifications on their use

The standard also provides guidance on environmental claims that should not be used. Declarations that are vague, nonspecific, or broadly imply an environmental benefit, such as "earth friendly" or "green," illustrate the kinds of claims that are deemed unacceptable.

ISO 14022 provides guidance on the appropriate use of symbols in self-declaration environmental claims. This standard recognizes that symbols associated with self-declaration claims may not have meaning other than that assigned by the manufacturer. Therefore, it sets out general principles for the use of environmental symbols. It also claims to standardize the meaning of symbols that are widely accepted as representative of environmentally benign products, although the mobius loop is the only such symbol currently included.

ISO 14023 will offer assistance with verification methodologies. As this book goes to press, a working draft has not yet been developed.

SC3 has decided to circulate all three self-declaration CDs for ballot together.

The fifth standard in the series, ISO 14024, *Type I guiding principles and procedures,* focuses on third-party, multiple-criteria environmental labeling programs. It is intended to provide practitioners and stakeholders with a reference document that ensures credibility and nondiscrimination.

The section on guiding principles and practices highlights 15 issues.

1. *Voluntary nature of the program*—environmental labeling programs developed by all organizations, even government agencies, must be voluntary.

2. *Relationship with regulations*—all products under consideration for an environmental label must comply with applicable environmental regulations.

3. *Life cycle consideration*—environmental labeling requirements should avoid the transfer of environmental burdens from one stage of the product life cycle to another or from one medium to another.

4. *Selectivity*—products receiving an environmental label must demonstrate a significant difference in total environmental impact. Additionally, arbitrary cut-off levels designed to exclude a predetermined percentage of products from qualifying for a label cannot be used.

5. *Product environmental criteria*—criteria for product differentiation must be based on life cycle considerations, set at attainable levels, and reviewed at defined intervals to accommodate new technologies, products, and environmental information.

6. *Product function characteristics*—environmental labeling programs must consider the purpose of a product category and the degree to which specific products fit the stated purpose.

7. *Consultation*—parties affected by an environmental labeling program (stakeholders) must be given an opportunity to participate in the selection and review of product categories, environmental criteria, and function characteristics.

8. *Transparency*—information about product categories, environmental criteria, function characteristics, certification procedures, funding sources, and other related issues should be made available to stakeholders.

9. *International trade aspects*—environmental labeling programs must not restrict trade.

10. *Compliance*—product environmental criteria and function characteristics must be verifiable by program practitioners.

11. *Accessibility*—environmental labeling programs must be open to all potential licensees.

12. *Objectivity, impartiality, and scientific basis of product environmental criteria*—environmental labeling criteria must be scientifically based and impartial.

13. *Avoidance of conflict of interest*—programs must demonstrate that funding sources do not create undue influence.

14. *Costs and fees*—application, testing, administration, and other fees must be imposed equitably for all applicants.

15. *Confidentiality*—information obtained from applicants or other stakeholders must be protected.

ISO 14024 goes on to lay out a framework for establishing environmental labeling program requirements. Issues for consideration fall into six areas.

1. Consultation with stakeholders

2. Selection of product categories

3. Selection and development of product environmental criteria

4. Selection of product function characteristics

5. Reporting and publication

6. Modifications to product environmental criteria

The standard concludes by delineating certification procedures, including procedures for assessing and demonstrating compliance and licensing.

A sixth standard is slated for development. ISO 14025 will address certified eco-profile (type III) programs. This type of environmental label is analogous to the nutrition label that appears on food products. The nutrition label does not claim that a particular food product is better than another; it merely identifies the attributes (calories, fat, salt, vitamin content) by which the consumer can determine whether one product is preferable to another.

The type III label is similar. It provides information about specific environmental impact indicators and leaves it to the purchaser to decide which product is most environmentally preferable.

According to Scientific Certification Systems, an Oakland, California–based company that provides detailed environmental profiles of products and their packaging through certified eco-profiles (see Figure 2.2), type III labels represent a significant departure from type I eco-logos and type II environmental claims. Type III labels

- Are applicable to all products and categories

- Contain accurate, objective environmental information about products based on life cycle assessment

- Provide a scientific basis for defining environmental performance and improvement

SC4: Environmental Performance Evaluation

SC4 is an anomaly in the ISO process. Despite ISO's stated policy of harmonizing existing standards, ISO 14031 represents an effort to create a new standard rather than harmonize existing practices.

SC4 defines EPE as a process to measure, analyze, assess, report, and communicate an organization's environmental performance. It is intended as a tool that assists company management in understanding environmental performance; determining necessary actions to achieve environmental policies, objectives, and targets; and communicating with interested parties.

The standard delineates three areas in which EPE is appropriate.

1. *Management system*—As described by ISO 14031, the management system encompasses the people throughout an organization and their actions that have (or cause) environmental impact. EPE focuses on those procedures and practices related to *management* of the organization's environmental aspects.

2. *Operational system*—This evaluation area encompasses the design and operation of physical facilities and equipment. EPE focuses on the material and energy employed in the production of goods and provision of services.

3. *Environment*—The environment includes air, water, land, natural resources, plant and animal life, and human health. Although designated as an evaluation area, most organizations are unlikely to do more than consider the environment as the context within which management and operational system performance is assessed. Unlike the management and operational systems, whose performance is under

Source: Reprinted with permission from Scientific Certification Systems, Oakland, California.

Figure 2.2. Type III labels for trash bags and packaging.

the organization's control, the environment is affected by the results of organizational performance.

A key concept of management and operational system EPE is the environmental performance indicator (EPI). As defined by SC4, an EPI is a specific description (or measure) of environmental performance within an evaluation area.

EPIs are likely to differ from company to company. Their selection and use should reflect the environmental characteristics of specific objectives and targets, procedures, or other activities whose performance is of concern. An organization seeking EPIs for training might consider the training program itself (resources allocated to training, hours of training per employee, percentage of employees involved in training), results of training (acquired knowledge, reduction in incidents involving trained personnel), or both.

EPIs can reflect different kinds of data.

- *Absolute*—raw number without interpretation (for example, total tons of ammonium sulfate discharged per year).

- *Relative*—information that has been interpreted on the basis of a separate piece of information, such as units of production (for example, tons of ammonium sulfate discharged per ton of product).

- *Ratio*—information that has been interpreted on the basis of a percentage increase or decrease from a baseline year (for example, tons of ammonium sulfate during baseline year is 100 percent, tons during year two is 95 percent).

- *Aggregated*—individual pieces of information that are combined (for example, tons of ammonium sulfate discharged and tons of sulfur dioxide emitted can be combined to describe total tons of pollutants).

However, all EPIs should be understandable, relevant, and value-neutral.

SC4 has developed several annexes to ISO 14031 that provide explicit examples of EPIs. SC4's business plan proposes a pilot test to ensure that specific practices and environmental performance indicators are appropriate in a variety of organizational settings. It is anticipated that the final standard will be published during 1998 or 1999.

SC5: Life Cycle Assessment

SC5 is developing four LCA standards. Achieving consensus has proven difficult because LCA was created as a means of evaluating manufacturing efficiency, not as a method for evaluating the environmental impact of manufacturing activities.

ISO 14040, *Principles and framework,* establishes the four phases of an LCA study.

- *Goal and scope definition*

    —Goal of the study, which specifies the reasons for conducting the LCA and the audience to whom study results will be communicated

    —Scope of the study, which specifies the breadth of the LCA including the system functions being studied, inputs and outputs, and data quality requirements

- *Inventory analysis*—compiles and quantifies relevant inputs and outputs of a production system

- *Impact assessment*—evaluates the significance of potential environmental impacts using the results of the life cycle inventory analysis

- *Interpretation*—presents conclusions and recommendations drawn from the findings of the inventory analysis and impact assessment. (This differs from the terminology used by the Society of Environmental Toxicology and Chemistry, which refers to the fourth phase as *improvement assessment.*)

Key features of the LCA methodology are presented and include the following:

- The depth of detail and time frame of an LCA study may vary according to the goal and scope definition.

- LCA results should not be reduced to a single overall conclusion, because trade-offs can occur at different stages of the system life cycle.

- There is no single method for conducting LCAs. Flexibility is necessary to implement LCAs that reflect specific applications and user needs.

The remaining three standards address the four LCA phases delineated in ISO 14040. The standard on inventory analysis, ISO 14041, reflects the current state of the art in this area, yet allows for flexibility to accommodate scientific advances. It is written for persons directly involved in conducting LCAs rather than a general audience. Special requirements and guidelines are provided on the following:

• *Formulating the goal and scope of the study*—The definition of the goal and scope of an LCA provide the initial plan for conducting the study. Life cycle inventory (LCI) focuses on executing that plan.

• *Defining and modeling the system(s) to be analyzed*—One of the most important considerations in an LCI is a clear specification of the function that is fulfilled by the system to be studied. This allows the definition of a quantifiable functional unit that measures system performance.

• *Collecting and preparing data for impact assessment*—LCIs are data intensive; however, the procedures used for data collection will vary according to the system processes to be studied. Because data quality will affect the utility of LCI results, consideration should be given to

—The geographic area (local, regional, national, international) from which data should be collected

—The time period of interest (for example, within the last three years) and the interval within that time period (for example, quarterly)

—The nature of technology to be included (for example, actual process technology, weighted average of process technology mix, best available technology only)

Additional data quality considerations for comparative assertions include representativeness, consistency, and reproducibility.

• *Verifying/evaluating the reliability of obtained inventory results*—This validation process serves to identify anomalies and missing data. It also serves to allocate the system inputs (materials, energy) and outputs (products, wastes) to unit processes within the overall system.

• *Reporting the results of an inventory analysis*—LCI results should be transparent. In other words, sufficient details should be provided about methodology, system boundaries, data used, assumptions, and limitations of the specific application to ensure that readers are able to understand, interpret, and use the results in a manner consistent with the goal and scope of the study.

Annexes contain an example of a data collection sheet, a checklist of critical aspects of an LCA with accompanying guideline questions, and examples of seven different allocation procedures.

Less progress has been made on the two remaining LCA standards. The work group for impact assessment, ISO 14042, developed its first draft proposal in September 1995, more than two years after work was initiated on most of the ISO 14000 standards.

In this preliminary form, ISO 14042 acknowledges that the methodological and scientific frameworks for life cycle impact analysis (LCIA) are evolving. Therefore, the standard does not specify LCIA techniques, which are aimed at understanding and evaluating the magnitude and significance of environmental impacts based on life cycle inventory analysis. Rather, it attempts to provide guidance concerning the fundamental aspects of impact assessment that are applicable to all available LCIA methods.

Three sections are of particular interest. The first provides an overview of current development in the field of LCIA, which includes three elements.

1. *Classification* takes life cycle inventory data and groups them into general impact categories. Traditionally, these categories are resource depletion, human health, and ecological impacts. Specific subcategories may be identified.

2. *Characterization* relies on scientific knowledge about cause-and-effect relationships and quantifies the environmental impact of each category.

3. *Valuation* establishes the significance of identified environmental impacts.

The second section of ISO 14042 addresses issues for consideration in identifying an appropriate methodological approach. It must be sufficiently sophisticated to ensure that LCIA results are useful, yet not so detailed that unnecessary and time-consuming work is devoted to details that will not be used. The intended use of a LCA affects the way in which LCIA is approached. Where the LCA is intended as a comparative tool, LCIA analyzes inventory data in terms of potential environmental hazards and the need to prevent resource depletion and pollution. Where the LCA is an exploratory tool for a single product system, LCIA identifies which environmental intervention or pollutant emission may cause actual environmental hazards. Finally, where the LCA serves as an indicative tool, LCIA reflects a holistic analysis of a product's life cycle.

The third section presents a methodological approach, procedure, and data requirements for LCIA as a comparative, explorative, and indicative tool. This level of detail will assist those who conduct LCA studies.

ISO 14043 was also not initiated until recently. In November 1995, the work group on interpretation agreed to prepare a generic systematic procedure for interpreting information provided by inventory analysis and/or impact assessment of a system. Initially, the work group is studying different applications of LCA in order to identify different approaches to interpretation. Applications under review include using LCA as a tool in decision making, improving a product system, determining environmental aspects, and labeling schemes.

SC6: Terms and Definitions

SC6 is responsible for harmonizing the terms and definitions used by the various SCs and their work groups. Ultimately, SC6 will publish a standard; however, it is constrained by the pace at which the other SCs complete their work.

WG: Environmental Aspects in Product Standards

In addition to the standards being developed or planned by the SCs, a work group has been charged with developing a standard on EAPS. This standard is intended to help standards writers consider environmental aspects in addition to other criteria when they develop product standards. It emphasizes a life cycle approach and so must be flexible enough to reflect changes that occur in the SC5 standards. The IEC, ISO's sister organization, has developed a similar standard that addresses environmental aspects in electrotechnical products.

Chapter 3

National and Regional Concerns

The U.S. Technical Advisory Group to ISO/TC 207 has been steadfast in its position that a single international environmental management system standard is preferable to a multitude of national EMS standards. Worldwide recognition of ISO 14001 will enable multinational companies to deploy one EMS throughout all facilities, regardless of location. This chapter examines the potential application of ISO 14001 in Europe, Mexico, Japan, and the United States.

ISO 14000 in Europe

On July 10, 1993, the European Commission (EC) published its Eco-Management and Audit Regulation (EMAR), a regulation established to promote continuous improvement in the environmental performance of companies performing industrial activities, and accompanying Eco-Management and Audit Scheme (EMAS). Technically, EMAR refers to the written language of the regulation and EMAS to the systems approach that EMAR embodies; however, the terms tend to be used interchangeably. Figure 3.1 describes the EC legal instruments.

When EMAS came into force on April 10, 1995, it applied only to companies in the industry sectors of manufacturing, waste disposal, and power. In 1996, it broadened its scope to include transportation companies and municipalities. Participating organizations are expected to do the following:

- Establish and implement environmental policies, programs, and management systems at individual operating sites.

- Systematically and objectively evaluate the performance of established environmental policies, programs, and management systems on a periodic basis.

> • *Regulations*—applicable in every member nation; comparable to national laws
>
> • *Directives*—addressed to member nations; results to be achieved are binding, but national authorities are free to choose how they will be incorporated into national legislation
>
> • *Decisions*—binding on those to whom they are addressed (such as a government or company)

Figure 3.1. EC legal instruments.

• Provide information about environmental performance to the public.

Since publication of the regulation, Europe's standardization body, Comité Européen de Normalisation (CEN), has attempted to determine whether to recognize existing national EMS standards as meeting the requirements of EMAS. Of particular concern to organizations involved with ISO/TC 207 was whether CEN would so recognize ISO 14001.

Annex I of the regulation delineates specific requirements concerning environmental policies, programs, and management systems. With three exceptions, EMAS annex I requirements parallel those contained in ISO 14001 (see section III for a comparison of these two standards). Those requirements are the following:

• Preparation of an annual environmental statement for each participating site. Specific information that must be contained in the statement includes

—An assessment of all significant environmental issues

—A summary of the figures on pollutant emissions; waste generation; consumption of raw materials, energy, and water; noise; and other significant environmental aspects, as appropriate

—Other factors regarding environmental performance

—A presentation of the environmental policy, program, and management system

- Verification of environmental statements by accredited environmental verifiers.

- Dissemination of the validated statement to the public.

Because of the similarities between EMAS and ISO 14001, CEN has developed a bridge document that recognizes ISO 14001 plus some additional requirements to ensure that all elements of EMAS are addressed. The bridge document describes what an organization must do beyond ISO 14001 to meet EMAS (for example, it addresses initial environmental review, audit frequency, and an annual public environmental statement).

Should CEN decide to recognize ISO 14001, it will not do so officially until ISO 14001 is published as a final standard. Although ISO members approved the standard in August 1996, publication will occur sometime in the fall.

ISO 14000 in Mexico

Author's note: Richard Wells, President, The Lexington Group, has been extremely active in the introduction of ISO 14000 to Latin America. He has briefed Mexico's Secretary of the Environment and senior government and industry representatives on ISO 14000. In addition, Wells has advised the Mexican delegation to ISO/TC 207.

Following his participation in a February 1996, trilateral (Canada, United States, and Mexico) meeting on ISO 14000, Wells was asked by Mexico's president of the National Institute of Ecology to provide technical direction to an industry/government/stakeholder work group that is examining how Mexico will integrate its approach to regulatory and nonregulatory environmental management. Those activities were the basis for this section, which was written by Wells.

Mexico, like most developing countries, is a relative late-comer to the ISO 14000 process. It sent its first delegate to the ISO/TC 207 meetings in June 1995, and it was only after the June 1996 meeting that it set up an advisory group on ISO 14000. At this point, Mexico has established subcommittees to address environmental management systems, auditing, environmental performance evaluation, and terms and definitions. It has not yet established committees to address life cycle analysis and labeling. It concurs with the view of other developing countries, however, that the life cycle analysis standard requires concepts and methodologies that are not available in developing countries and may act as nontariff trade barriers, keeping developing-country companies out of major international markets.

To understand the impact of ISO 14000 in Mexico, it is necessary to understand that the Mexican economy is divided into at least three components. So-called "micro" companies with 15 or fewer employees constitute 92 percent of the industrial enterprises in Mexico. These companies operate within a purely domestic setting and are extremely unlikely to be affected by ISO 14000. The important effects of ISO 14000 will be among small firms (16 to 100 employees) and medium and large firms (more than 100 employees). The effects on the latter two categories of firms are likely to be extremely different and need to be examined.

Effects on Large Firms and Multinationals

Large firms and multinationals located in Mexico will be affected by the same forces that influence their counterparts in other countries. A significant difference from other countries may be that firms located in Mexico have fewer alternative mechanisms to demonstrate environmental improvement. While a developed-country company may be able to document its environmental performance in the absence of an ISO 14000–certified management system, a Mexican company operating at the same level may find it advantageous to be able to demonstrate conformance to an internationally certified standard.

As in other countries, numerous large Mexican companies are evaluating what steps they should take with respect to ISO 14000. For the most part, their attitude has been to wait and see, but there is recognition that Mexico will need to adapt to the international marketplace. A director of a major Mexican company and a leader among senior managers, concerned about environmental issues, recently described two alternative courses for ISO 14000 in his company and in Mexico more generally. Taking a negative view of ISO 9000, he said that ISO 14000 could become, like ISO 9000, evidence of a highly developed bureaucratic management system. In that case, his company would continue to develop its own environmental management systems, which are already based on a total quality management model. Following what it has done with ISO 9000, it will add to its existing system those elements it needs for certification if it sees a commercial advantage in doing so. It will not, however, use ISO 14000 as the basis for the development of its internal management system.

This view reflects a quite negative experience with ISO 9000 in Mexico as a bureaucratic requirement and a concern that ISO 14000 will be interpreted as ISO 9000 applied to the environment. Since the individual in question is one of Mexico's corporate leaders on environmental management, his views cannot be taken lightly. Mexico has not been involved in the development of the ISO 14000 standard, and it is vulnerable to the interpretation of ISO 14000 in highly bureaucratic terms by foreign certification firms. In this case, ISO 14000 becomes a necessary evil—a cost companies incur because it is required to gain, increase, or maintain access to the international market—but not a means of improving environmental performance.

The alternative scenario described by the same individual is more hopeful, but depends on strong leadership from government agencies and industry. In this scenario, the ISO 14000 series standards are seen as a reasonable model for environmental management, distilling international experience to a set of core elements. This international experience can provide an effective model for a corporate environmental management system. The point here is that ISO 14000 can serve as a viable model for environmental management system improvement system that can be adopted whether or not an organization takes the next step toward certification.

Clearly, the challenge among large companies is to influence the implementation of ISO 14000 to focus on its potential to improve environmental management systems. Large companies are extremely concerned about the development of additional paperwork burdens that do not directly add value. This is a particularly important concern, given their experience with both ISO 9000 and Mexico's environmental enforcement system, which is extremely paperwork oriented.

An advantage of ISO 14001 as a model for large Mexican companies is that it fits with efforts already underway to develop environmental management systems. Unlike U.S. companies that have developed an environmental management structure oriented around a command-and-control regulatory system over a period of several decades, Mexican companies have an opportunity to develop management systems using ISO 14001 and 14004 as a model. This approach will allow for more flexible systems that are better integrated in corporate operations.

A recent survey of Mexican industry funded by the World Bank suggests that the process of developing management systems is well underway. For example, the survey indicates that 73 percent of large companies have written environmental policies, 74 percent have procedures in place to identify the environmental aspects of their operations, and 57 percent have environmental plans with specific objectives and targets. Senior management at 28 percent of these companies ascribes a very high priority to environmental issues, and at 54 percent of companies, senior management gives environmental issues a high priority.

Another important advantage of ISO 14000 for large companies is its linkage to Mexico's emerging regulatory structure. In the United States, ISO 14000 is being regarded as an alternative to regulation; that is, as a substitute for elements of a command-and-control regulatory structure that are already in place. In Mexico, environmental regulations are being developed and there exists an opportunity to design regulations as a complement to voluntary industry initiatives, including ISO 14000. At a trilateral meeting on ISO 14000 in January 1991, Francisco Giner de los Rios, the director of regulation within Mexico's National Institute of Ecology, expressed his intention to design regulations that set a floor rather than a target and to rely on voluntary standards and market mechanisms to develop flexible environmental improvement projects.

One substantial danger in the ISO 14000 process from the viewpoint of large companies in Mexico concerns its relationship with other voluntary programs. Recently, Mexico's environmental enforcement agency promulgated Terms of Reference for a Voluntary Environmental Audit Program. Companies that undertake voluntary audits receive some recognition for having undergone an audit. More importantly, they receive some relief from frequent regulatory inspections and receive a grace period during which they can rectify deficiencies noted in the audit. Thus, the environmental audit program is an important alternative to a rigid, paperwork-driven regulatory enforcement system.

Many Mexican companies, however, feel that the voluntary audit program is missing an important opportunity in not being more closely tied to ISO 14001. The certification procedures involved for voluntary audits are not substantially different from those anticipated for ISO 14001, and in some areas the two programs cover similar topics. In particular, Part E of the Terms of Reference addresses environmental management systems. The fact that voluntary audits are not coordinated means that companies will have to meet duplicative requirements if they wish to participate in both programs or that they will have less incentive to participate in either program because they do not receive the benefits of both programs. A Mexican CEO recently pointed to his company's voluminous submission for a voluntary audit and said, "See all that? We will have to do it all over again for ISO 14000."

The example of voluntary audits illustrates the issues Mexican industry and government will face in addressing the interface between ISO 14000 and government programs. Multiple government agencies, each with their own perspective, will need to work with industry and stakeholder groups to design companies that are acceptable to all parties. At least three government agencies will be involved: the Attorney General for Environmental Protection (enforcement), the National Institute for Ecology (environmental policy and standards), and the Directorate of Standards within the Department of Commerce and Industrial Development. In addition, industrial associations that have a powerful voice in Mexico will be concerned about reducing paperwork burdens, and stakeholder groups will be concerned about preventing the self-regulatory elements in ISO 14000 from being used as a pretext for backsliding from Mexico's commitment to environmental improvement.

Effects on Small Companies

If the large company issues are daunting, the small company issues are more so. Unlike large companies, small companies have not developed the management systems elements that will allow them to adapt rapidly to ISO 14001. In the same survey that identified fairly widespread use by large companies of management systems elements specified in ISO 14001, small companies were shown to be about one-third as likely to have key management system elements as large companies. For example, only 18 percent of small companies have environmental policies, and 16 percent have environmental plans incorporating objectives and targets. Fewer than 10 percent of small companies provide environmental training to their nonenvironmental employees, and senior management ascribes a very high priority to environmental issues at only 8 percent of small companies. Note, moreover, that by virtue of being small, a small company is already in the top decile of companies in Mexico: 92 percent of Mexico's industrial enterprises are micro enterprises, with fewer than 16 employees.

The condition of small company environmental management systems is behind Giner's statement that ISO 14000 could become an internal barrier to trade within Mexico. Given the state of their environmental management systems, small companies are unlikely to be able to upgrade their systems at any time in the near future to meet the requirements of ISO 14001. Giner argues that to the extent that major foreign purchasers in sectors such as electronics and autos come to require certification of their suppliers, small companies may find themselves systematically excluded from the most dynamic and rapidly growing sector of the economy—the export sector. This scenario is not likely to come into being in the short term, but it may take place over the longer term if ISO 14001 meets its goal of providing a widespread standard of environmental management.

At the same time, ISO 14001 presents an opportunity to improve environmental management systems among small companies. The systems specified by ISO can become the basis for cost-effective small company management systems so long as it is recognized that they should be appropriate to the nature and scale of the organization's operations. Paradoxically also, because small companies have small or nonexistent environmental staffs, environmental considerations are generally better integrated into facility operations. For example, small companies are more likely than larger companies to have environmental managers drawn from facility management or operations.

Conclusion

Several conclusions arise from a February 1996 trilateral North American Free Trade Agreement meeting in Mexico City on ISO 14000 sponsored by the U.S. Council of International Business, the Canadian Chamber of Commerce, and Mexico's Confederation of Industrial Chambers. Among these is the fact that Mexico is at a crossroads relative to its lack of participation in the development of the ISO 14001 and 14004 documents and that it must now interpret these documents and apply them to the Mexican context. As suggested in this chapter, this context differs substantially from that found in the United States or Europe. Moreover, Mexico is more vulnerable, again because of its lack of in-depth knowledge of the documents, to interpretation of consultants and accreditation firms who equate ISO 9000 and ISO 14000.

On the other hand, the ISO 14000 series environmental management system model presents an opportunity to upgrade environmental management using a flexible, cost-effective management model. If not the last, ISO 14001 and 14004 are certainly the best chance to date to elevate environmental management to a corporate priority and to couple industrial initiatives, stakeholder concerns, and government regulation in a coherent national environmental policy.

ISO 14000 in Japan

Japan, still smarting from its decision not to advocate ISO 9000 certification, appears to have embraced ISO 14000. In mid-1995, before the draft standard had been distributed for balloting as a final ISO standard, several companies announced that they were developing strategies to implement ISO 14001 by early 1996.

The Toyota Motor Corporation's manager of international public affairs has stated publicly that the company plans to enhance existing environmental control systems by implementing ISO 14001 in all facilities beginning in 1996.[1] At this point, the company does not plan to pursue certification. Instead, Toyota will rely on self-declaration until such time as certification is perceived to offer a competitive advantage.

Two electronics companies also initiated efforts to implement ISO 14001 in 1995. Matsushita Electric Industrial Company and Omron Corporation also are pursuing ISO 14001 aggressively.[2] Matsushita, whose brands include Panasonic and Quasar, has revised its corporate environmental policy to require that all its facilities conform to the standard. Similarly, Omron, a manufacturer of automatic teller machines, plans to certify all of its facilities within the next three years.

More recently, the Ministry of International Trade and Industry announced that it plans to ask companies to incorporate ISO 14001 into existing environmental management methods.[3] This request parallels the decision of the Japanese Industrial Standards Committee to adopt ISO 14001 as soon as it is published as a final ISO standard. Experts suggest that most existing environmental management systems in large companies conform to ISO 14001 requirements.

EMS in the United States

With the publication of ISO 14001, U.S. companies may have two similar EMS standards from which to select. ANSI is considering adoption of ISO 14001 as the U.S. national EMS standard. NSF International has been registering companies to its own EMS standard, NSF 110.

ANSI and ISO 14001

In March 1995, the U.S. TAG to ISO/TC 207 agreed that ANSI should pursue "synchronization" of ISO 14001 and its adoption as a U.S. national standard.[4] As used in this context, synchronization refers to timing, not harmonization.

ANSI designated three standards development organizations— ASTM, ASQC, and NSF International—to work collectively on determining U.S. support for adoption of ISO 14001 as the U.S. national EMS standard. Ultimately, the U.S. adoption of ISO 14001 will occur under the auspices of ANSI's Z-1 committee.

According to ANSI procedures, comments concerning adoption of international standards are solicited from groups such as the TAG and its own members. Ballots submitted to U.S. TAG members overwhelmingly supported adoption of ISO 14001. This outcome reinforced the position taken by the TAG when ISO/TC 207 began its work in June 1993—there should be only one international standard, in lieu of multiple national and regional standards.

Additionally, ANSI's Board of Standards Review must ensure that ANSI procedures were followed during development of ISO 14001. Because ISO/TC 207 employed a consensus process and addressed dissenting comments, it is likely that the ISO/TC 207 procedures will be accepted by ANSI. ANSI's TC 207 program administrator has indicated that if the Board of Standards Review is satisfied with the ISO/TC 207 procedures, ISO 14001 will be adopted verbatim as an American National Standard.[5]

Publication of an American National Standard on EMS is largely symbolic. ISO 14001 can be implemented by U.S. organizations regardless of its status as an American standard.

NSF International and EMS

NSF International, a standards development organization known for its work in the public health arena, also provides third-party standardization services in systems management, including environmental management and quality management. In 1995, NSF published NSF 110, *Environmental Management Systems—Guiding Principles and Generic Requirements.*

At that time, NSF planned to submit NSF 110 to ANSI for consideration as the American National Standard for EMS. This was met with fairly strong resistance by many in the U.S. TAG, who felt that such a move undermined the U.S. position concerning a single international standard.

NSF, therefore, agreed not to submit the standard to ANSI. With the EPA's financial support, however, it initiated a pilot project in which 18 companies from a variety of industries assessed the usefulness of the two standards. See section III for an element-by-element comparison of the two standards.

Notes

1. "Japanese Firms Preparing for ISO 14001 Implementation," *International Environmental Systems Update* 2, no. 9 (September 1995): 7–8.

2. Ibid.

3. "Trade Ministry Asks Firms to Prepare for ISO 14000." In *The ISO 14000 Handbook,* edited by Joseph Cascio (Fairfax, Va.: CEEM Information Services and Milwaukee: ASQC Quality Press, 1996), 478–481.

4. Agreed by consensus at March 6–7 U.S. TAG meeting; later supported by written ballot in January 1996.

5. Presentation at U.S. TAG meetings March 6–7 and September 14–15, 1995.

Section II

Executing ISO 14001

Chapter 4

Why to Implement ISO 14001

Although national environmental management standards and industry environmental codes of practice have proliferated in recent years, an international environmental management standard offers a number of advantages to domestic and multinational companies alike. As is true for all ISO standards, the creation of ISO 14001 was through consensus of interested parties from nearly 50 countries. Delegates and experts were guided by the following concepts.

• A standard that is unduly burdensome defeats two major benefits of standardization: simplicity and reduced cost. Rather than providing something completely new, ISO 14001 reflects the best practices that exist in a variety of settings. The 17 elements incorporate components that are found in a number of standards and codes of practice.

• Public disclosure is an internal management decision to be made by individual companies. Conformity to ISO 14001 does not empower individual stakeholders, organizations, or other external interested parties with the right to obtain sensitive information. Requiring such disclosure is outside the purview of the standard and does not further ISO's goal of improving environmental management.

• ISO standards are not intended to serve as substitutes for or supplements to national laws and regulations. Therefore, ISO 14001 does not establish specific performance levels and rates of improvement. The standard provides a framework that allows individual companies the latitude to establish their own policies and performance objectives.

• Third-party verification of conformity to the standard is not required. Organizations have the option to self-audit and self-declare the adoption of ISO 14001.

Uses of ISO 14001

According to the Scope section of ISO 14001, the standard is applicable to any organization that wishes to accomplish the following:

- Implement, maintain, and improve an environmental management system.
- Assure itself of its conformance with its stated environmental policy.
- Demonstrate such conformance to others.
- Seek certification/registration of its EMS by an external organization.
- Make a self-determination and self-declaration of conformance with the standard.

It is anticipated that the implementation and continual improvement of the EMS will result in improved environmental performance. It is important to understand that conformity to ISO 14001 does not guarantee better environmental performance. The standard merely provides the structure within which companies will establish, achieve, and control whatever level of environmental performance they set for themselves.

The standard also allows companies the flexibility to implement an EMS within whatever boundaries are deemed most appropriate. A company can apply ISO 14001 as broadly or narrowly as it chooses, from the entire organization to divisions, individual operating units, or specific activities.

Benefits of ISO 14001

The benefits of implementing ISO 14001 are as varied as the organizations that have elected to conform to the standard. To paraphrase a well-known expression, some companies will achieve all benefits, all companies will achieve some benefits, but not all companies will achieve all benefits. The nature of a company's operations; the regulations with which it must comply; and its traditional approach to addressing changing customer demands, emerging technologies, and capital investments will influence the areas in which the greatest benefits are derived.

The most significant benefits fall into three areas.

1. *Assurance of policy implementation*—Many companies have had the experience of devoting time and resources to the development of an environmental policy and displaying it where it will be seen by visitors and guests, only to discover that it has little effect on the way in which various operating units function on a day-to-day basis. ISO 14001 forces organizations to overcome inertia by linking the policy to articulated objectives and targets.

Making the environmental policy one of the two key elements on which the EMS is based (environmental aspects is the other) yields two outcomes. First, the policy tends to be meaningful in terms of an organization's operations and activities. The need to develop objectives and targets that contribute to the achievement of the policy prevent companies from making empty promises.

Second, the requirement for top management review to ascertain the possible need for changes to the environmental policy ensures that the policy will be viable despite changing company circumstances.

2. *Worldwide consistency for multinational companies*—ISO 14001 provides a mechanism for operating in an environmentally responsible manner in locations where local standards are minimal or do not exist. ISO 14001 does not export any country's environmental requirements to another; rather, it provides an internally consistent approach to environmental concerns.

Implementation of ISO 14001 has the potential to distinguish companies as environmentally concerned business partners throughout the world. It is likely to be a valuable asset in working with host governments that are interested in establishing regulatory frameworks based on performance rather than prescriptive, command-and-control requirements.

3. *Customer satisfaction*—There is little question that most companies will implement ISO 14001 in response to demand from key customers. U.S. manufacturers of nondurable consumer goods are unlikely to be pressured to implement the standard because most American consumers are unfamiliar with either ISO or the concept of environmental management. However, original equipment manufacturers will be influenced strongly by the industry sectors that they serve. For example, a decision by U.S. auto manufacturers to favor

suppliers who can demonstrate conformity to ISO 14001 would have implications for providers of aluminum, plastics, electronics, and steel.

Other benefits include the following.

• *Reduced costs*—ISO 14001's emphasis on prevention of pollution can reduce costs in two ways: decreased expenditures on raw materials and decreased waste disposal costs. Efforts to prevent pollution encourage attention to the toxicity of materials used in operating processes and other activities. This can result in more efficient use of toxic materials or their elimination through material substitution.

When toxic materials are used more efficiently or replaced, the environmental impact of process waste streams is lessened. Less waste, in turn, results in reduced costs associated with treatment, transport, and disposal.

Costs savings also may be realized in reduced fines and/or penalties. EPA's self-policing policy, discussed in the next section, provides relief under certain circumstances for companies that have implemented an EMS.

• *Improved public image*—It is difficult to quantify the impact of public perception. However, companies report that local citizens and community groups react positively to the news that ISO 14001 is being implemented.

This reaction contrasts sharply with the position taken by a small number of environmental special-interest groups. Although some environmental groups support the objectives of ISO 14001, others have been critical that it does not go far enough.

• *Improved relations with regulatory agencies*—State departments of environmental protection have reacted to ISO 14001 with varying degrees of interest. While most states are taking a wait-and-see attitude, a handful have indicated that ISO 14001 certification has the potential to serve as a substitute for certain regulatory requirements. As this book goes to press, several states have invited company participation in pilot studies to determine the effectiveness of ISO 14001 in fulfilling various permit and other environmental operating requirements.

Equally compelling is the level of interest expressed by the EPA through a variety of proposals and pilot projects.

> —EPA's Office of Wastewater Management has developed a proposal to encourage the use of ISO 14001 in the National

Pollution Discharge Elimination System permit program. The proposal suggests that companies certified to ISO 14001 would be subject to less frequent reporting requirements.

—The Environmental Leadership Program, a pilot project to explore mechanisms for creating environmental excellence within companies, requires participants to address EMS issues and encouraged proposals that identified a link to ISO 14001.

—An EPA Region I (New England) initiative known as 3PC has attempted to link compliance audit and pollution prevention programs to ISO 14001.

—Project XL provides responsible companies with an opportunity to demonstrate how "alternative strategies," such as ISO 14001, can result in environmental performance that surpasses the levels achieved by simple compliance with applicable laws and regulations.

These efforts are notable because they represent an effort by the EPA to be more flexible about the kinds of voluntary approaches that companies might use to achieve regulatory compliance.

U.S. Company Concerns

A concern that is expressed by many U.S. companies contemplating the adoption of ISO 14001 concerns the potential for fines and penalties if a voluntary effort to improve environmental management reveals a violation that otherwise would not have come to light. The EPA's response to this concern is embodied in its policy on self-policing.

EPA's Self-Audit Policy

In April 1995, the EPA developed an interim audit policy[1] "to provide incentives for regulated entities that conduct voluntary compliance evaluations and also disclose and correct violations." However, this policy did not favor privilege and immunity; it stated that an environmental audit privilege "could be misused to shield bad actors or to frustrate access to crucial factual information."

In January 1996, the EPA's final policy on Incentives for Self-Policing: Discovery, Disclosure, Correction, and Prevention of Violations went into effect.[2] This policy is intended to enhance protection of human health and the environment by encouraging regulated entities to voluntarily discover, disclose, and correct violations of environmental requirements.

In an effort to encourage voluntary identification of violations, the EPA's policy offers several incentives.

• *Elimination of gravity-based penalties*—EPA's audit policy waives gravity-based penalties for violations under two sets of conditions.

> —Those that are discovered through voluntary audits and promptly disclosed and corrected

> —Those found through documented procedures for self-policing where the company can demonstrate a compliance management program (such as might be developed under ISO 14001 section 4.5.1)

Penalties reflect two elements. The economic benefit portion represents a defendant's economic gain from noncompliance. The gravity-based portion is punitive.

The EPA's audit policy retains the right to recover economic benefit penalties for two reasons: It provides an incentive to comply on time, and it protects responsible companies from being undercut by their noncomplying competitors.

• *Reduction of gravity-based penalties*—For companies that discover, disclose, and correct violations, but do not have an effective compliance management program, gravity-based penalties will be reduced by 75 percent. The intent of this reduction is to encourage companies to work with the EPA to resolve environmental problems and begin to develop an effective compliance management program.

• *No recommendations for criminal prosecution*—EPA will not recommend criminal prosecution for a company that uncovers violations through environmental audits or due diligence, and promptly discloses and expeditiously corrects those violations. This incentive is limited to good actors and, therefore, has important limitations. EPA reserves the right to recommend prosecution for the criminal conduct of any culpable individual.

In order to qualify for these incentives, nine specified conditions must be met. Failure to fulfill these conditions means that the incentives do not apply.

1. The violation was discovered through an environmental audit or an objective, documented systematic procedure or practice.

2. The violation was identified voluntarily.

3. The regulated entity fully discloses the violation within 10 days (or less if required by law) in writing to the EPA.

4. The violation must be discovered and disclosed independent of government or third-party plaintiff.

5. The regulated entity corrects the violation within 60 days and certifies in writing that the violation has been corrected.

6. The regulated entity agrees in writing to take steps to prevent a recurrence of the violation.

7. The specific violation has not occurred previously within the past three years at the same facility, or is not part of a pattern of violations by the parent organization within the past five years.

8. The violation did not result in serious actual harm to human health or the environment or violate the specific terms of any judicial or administrative order or consent decree.

9. The regulated entity cooperates as requested by the EPA.

State Audit Policies

In contrast to the EPA, which does not want to provide privilege for audit information, 17 states have enacted laws that provide for environmental audit privilege and/or environmental audit immunity.[3] Although several states have rejected such measures, more than 12 other states are considering similar legislation.

None of these state laws address EMS audit data specifically. However, these laws are intended to protect companies that seek out and correct instances of noncompliance. ISO 14001 audits are not compliance audits, and it is an open question whether state courts would extend privilege to EMS audits.

According to several environmental attorneys, companies conducting ISO 14001 audits in states with environmental audit privilege laws should not assume that their audits are protected. The attorney–client privilege covers communications made in confidence between attorneys and their clients in order to provide or obtain candid legal advice. Attorneys suggest that it will be hard for companies to argue that ISO 14001 audits are conducted to secure legal advice. ISO 14001 audits are likely to be conducted in order to gain a competitive advantage because a company wants or needs to demonstrate that it meets the standard.

The attorney work product doctrine also is unlikely to provide protection. Attorney work product pertains to materials that are treated as confidential and prepared under the supervision of legal counsel in anticipation of litigation. The results of ISO 14001 audits are likely to be widely distributed within the company, to customers, and to other interested external parties. Further, few such audits, if any, are likely to be conducted in anticipation of litigation.

Privilege for audit results appears to provide little, if any, protection for companies that conduct EMS audits and, in fact, runs counter to the intended management objectives of implementing ISO 14001.

The more compelling issue for companies is immunity. Companies that attempt to continually improve their environmental management systems and, by extension, environmental performance, should not be sanctioned when the process reveals violations. There is a need to ensure that companies that elect to implement ISO 14001 are no worse off than those who do not.

Companies that are exploring the implications of implementing ISO 14001 should consider the following issues as part of their decision-making process.

• Confidentiality issues will vary with the type and intended purpose of ISO 14001 documentation.

• Most organizations will rely on existing information, much of which may be reported to state and federal agencies under various statutory requirements. If documented procedures incorporate legally required data, privilege may be irrelevant.

• The only mandatory disclosure required by ISO 14001 is the environmental policy. Existing laws and regulations require disclosure of an array of data. Companies need to determine what additional information might become part of the ISO 14001 audit and whether privilege is an issue.

• Companies have considerable control over the level of documentation and how it is maintained. Those who are concerned about privilege can craft the EMS to put in the least amount of sensitive data and still fulfill the requirements of ISO 14001.

• An ISO 14001 audit examines the environmental management system only. It is neither an environmental compliance nor performance audit.

• ISO 14001 audit working papers and findings are owned by the company that commissioned the audit.

ISO 14001 Registration

The terms *registration* and *certification* are often used synonymously. Certification is the preferred term in Europe. In the United States, certifications carry specific liability implications; therefore, the preferred term in that country is *registration*.

Registration can be thought of as a three-tiered process that is initiated when the company seeking registration submits an application to a registrar. Registrars can be accredited; those that are use certified auditors to conduct conformity assessments. Accreditation schemes for ISO 14000 are likely to be similar to those established for ISO 9000. The Registrar Accreditation Board and ANSI are currently structuring a joint ISO 14000 accreditation program.

Companies should select a registrar with the same diligence that is applied to the acquisition of other business services. Registrar experience in the company's industry should be a primary consideration. Other factors could include the registrar's reputation and that of its accrediting body, the experience of auditors assigned to the conformity assessment, and cost.

The second tier is performance of a conformity assessment. The registrar will evaluate the company's EMS to ascertain whether it fulfills all the requirements of ISO 14001. Such assessments generally entail a review of relevant written policies, procedures, documents, and records (often referred to as a *desktop audit*), followed by an on-site assessment. Deficiencies—that is, identified nonconformities with the ISO 14001 requirements—are reported to the company. Once the company has completed corrective action, the audit team will recommend acceptance for or denial of registration to the registrar.

The third and final step is award of a certificate to the applicant company. ISO 9000 certificates are effective for three years, at which time companies must reregister. It is anticipated that ISO 14000 registrars will adhere to a similar schedule.

Today, the majority of U.S. companies implementing ISO 14001 assert that they are doing so for internal management purposes only. Those that anticipate the need to demonstrate conformance to the standard plan to self-declare. Few have expressed a willingness to pursue formal registration, although it is likely that customer preference for third-party audits in lieu of self-declaration will spur interest.

Notes

1. Environmental Protection Agency, "Incentives for Self-Policing: Discovery, Disclosure, Correction, and Prevention of Violations." *Federal Register* 60, no. 246 (December 22, 1995): 66706–66712.

2. Ibid.

3. These states are Arkansas, Colorado, Idaho, Illinois, Indiana, Kansas, Kentucky, Michigan, Minnesota, Mississippi, New Hampshire, Oregon, South Dakota, Texas, Utah, Virginia, and Wyoming.

Chapter 5

Understanding ISO 14001

Companies contemplating the implementation of ISO 14001 are well-advised to assess their existing environmental management system in order to identify activities that fulfill ISO 14001 requirements and gaps that must be filled. As a result of the multitude of federal and state environmental regulations and the array of industry environmental codes of practice to which various organizations subscribe, many U.S. companies are well on their way to achieving conformity with ISO 14001.

If an EMS assessment is to be useful, a thorough understanding of ISO 14001 elements is essential. This chapter discusses each element in the standard. Chapter 6 raises questions that should be answered and suggests sources of information and data that can offer objective evidence for determining the extent to which a company's existing EMS conforms to ISO 14001.

ISO 14001 is organized into five sections and three annexes; see appendix A for the complete text of the standard. An unnumbered introduction provides a brief overview of the importance of environmental management and the purpose of the standard. This is followed by numbered sections 1, Scope; 2, Normative References; and 3, Definitions. None of these sections is considered part of the EMS specification.

Section 4, Environmental Management System Requirements, contains the elements that must be established, implemented, and maintained in order to conform to ISO 14001. Companies seeking certification will be audited against this section only.

Annex A offers guidance on the use of the specification. It provides additional information that is intended to clarify the intent of the standard. It does not impose any additional certification requirements and is not auditable for certification.

49

Annexes B and C contain a table that compares ISO 14001 elements with those of ISO 9001 and a bibliography, respectively. Like Annex A, they are informative only and do not impose additional EMS requirements.

It is absolutely critical to understand that ISO 14001 is an environmental *management* standard, not an environmental *performance* standard. Therefore, assessing the degree of fit between an existing EMS and ISO 14001 should emphasize procedures and practices.

Clause 4.2, Environmental Policy

Top management shall define the organization's environmental policy and ensure that it

a) is appropriate to the nature, scale and environmental impacts of its activities, products or services;

b) includes a commitment to continual improvement and prevention of pollution;

c) includes a commitment to comply with relevant environmental legislation and regulations, and with other requirements to which the organization subscribes;

d) provides the framework for setting and reviewing environmental objectives and targets;

e) is documented, implemented and maintained and communicated to all employees;

f) is available to the public.

Many companies purport to have an environmental policy. Typically, such policy statements assert that the company will comply with all applicable laws and regulations, protect the health and safety of employees, and safeguard the environment. Figure 5.1 contains typical policy statements.

ISO 14001 defines the *environmental policy* as a statement of a company's intentions and principles in relation to its overall environmental performance, which provides a framework for establishing objectives and targets. Moreover, ISO 14001 requires that the environmental

The most common themes are regulatory compliance, employee safety and health, environmental stewardship, and leadership. Examples of typical policy statements are as follows:

- ZZZ is committed to meeting all applicable laws and regulatory requirements.

- ZZZ is committed to providing a safe and healthy work environment for all employees.

- ZZZ is committed to managing all operations in an environmentally responsible manner.

- It is the policy of ZZZ to manage all phases of our operations to minimize adverse effects on the environment and the safety and health of our employees.

- ZZZ is committed to achieving recognition as an industrial leader in employee safety and health and environmental protection.

Figure 5.1. Common themes in corporate environmental policies.

policy include four specific requirements. These commitments are to the following:

- Compliance with relevant environmental legislation and regulations

- Compliance with other requirements to which the organization voluntarily subscribes

- Continual improvement

- Prevention of pollution

The environmental policy must meet the following requirements.

- *Be documented.* It is important to ascertain where the policy appears. Some companies display their policies in public areas, such as the building reception area; others distribute it as an internal document in various forms.

- *Be implemented and maintained.* Organizations must effect the transition from words on paper to concrete actions that transform the policy into a guiding document that influences daily business conduct.

- *Be communicated to all employees.* Management must convey the meaning of the policy to employees throughout the organization. This can be done through a variety of mechanisms such as new employee orientation, videotapes and audiotapes, and written statements. Equally important is determining whether employees understand the policy. This is best assessed by going directly to the source and asking employees whether they are familiar with the company's environmental policy.

External communication is also required. ISO 14001 states that the environmental policy must be available to the public. At the very least, this requires some mechanism to respond to such information requests. More proactive companies will disseminate such information to targeted constituencies, for example, shareholders, customers, local community organizations, and state regulators.

Clause 4.3, Planning

The remaining elements of ISO 14001 are organized to reflect the Shewhart cycle, named for its creator, Walter A. Shewhart, a statistician at Bell Telephone Laboratories in New York. More commonly known as the PDCA cycle, for plan-do-check-act, it served as the foundation for W. Edwards Deming's management method.

The first step in the Shewhart cycle, plan, is to study a process in order to determine what changes might improve it. Conformity to ISO 14001 requires that planning encompass four components—identification of environmental aspects, understanding of legal and other requirements, establishment of objectives and targets, and creation of an environmental management program—to ensure fulfillment of the environmental policy.

4.3.1 Environmental Aspects

> The organization shall establish and maintain (a) procedure(s) to identify the environmental aspects of its activities, products or services that it can control and over which it can be expected to have an influence, in order to determine those which have or can have significant impacts on the environment. The organization shall ensure that the aspects related to these significant

impacts are considered in setting its environmental objectives.
     The organization shall keep this information up-to-date.

This requirement constitutes one of the most misunderstood sections of ISO 14001. As defined in section 3.3, an environmental aspect is any element of an organization's activities, products, or services that can interact with the environment (for example, the use of lead in the manufacture of steel). An environmental impact is any change in the environment as a result of the aspect (for example, lead dust). Figure 5.2 illustrates the distinction between environmental aspects and impacts for a manufacturing process, a product, and a service. ISO 14001 requires that the organization have a procedure to identify its environmental aspects and their impacts. Those aspects associated with *significant* environmental impacts are to be *considered* in the development of objectives and targets. When assessing an EMS for conformity to ISO 14001, actual or potential environmental aspects and their impacts are secondary to the procedures by which such aspects are identified and their impacts evaluated.

Growth in the number of environmental regulations (more than 13,000 pages in Title 40 of the U.S. Code of Federal Regulations) has provided U.S. companies a distinct advantage in fulfilling this requirement. Most significant environmental aspects and impacts are identified by regulations and, therefore, recognized and addressed by organizations. This boon, however, is a double-edged sword. By relying

	Process	Product	Service
Example	Manufacture of acrylonitrile monomer	Styrofoam coffee cup	Lawn maintenance
Aspect	Ammonium sulfate	Not degradable or recyclable	Application of herbicides and pesticides
Impact	Injection of ammonium sulfate into deep wells	Landfill	Nonpoint source pollution

Figure 5.2. Examples of environmental aspects and impacts.

on regulations to identify significant environmental aspects, companies have not needed to develop their own procedures. Faced with the need to identify environmental aspects beyond the purview of environmental regulations, companies of all sizes are scrambling to develop internal procedures that will withstand scrutiny.

The most typical approach to identification of environmental aspects involves examination of individual processes. Because every process is bounded by the discrete parameters of inputs (such as materials, energy), a value-added transformation, and outputs (such as finished product, reusable materials, wastes), a procedure for identification of environmental aspects is rendered straightforward and manageable.

Depending on the nature of the specific operation under review, consideration usually is given to the following:

- Air emissions
- Water discharges
- Soil contamination
- Use of raw materials
- Use of natural resources

The standard is not intended, and should not be interpreted, to require a detailed life cycle assessment. Nor do companies need to evaluate each product, component, or raw material input. Annex A indicates that companies may select categories of activities, products, or services to identify those aspects most likely to have a significant impact.

Less common, but no less important, is identification of the environmental aspects associated with planned activities, such as construction, changes in operations, and clean-up projects.

Once the organization has identified its environmental aspects, it must determine their impact on the environment. A *significant* environmental aspect is one that has or can have a significant environmental impact. Significant environmental aspects are intended to be the focus of objectives and targets and, therefore, of improved environmental performance.

Environmental impacts can be acute or chronic. Acute impacts are associated with episodic or short-term events, such as an accidental oil tanker spill. Chronic impacts result from long-term events, such as improper disposal of used oil by car owners. Typically, environmental impact is assessed by estimating its

- *Likelihood.* This will vary according to the status of the operation or process under review. Therefore, the organization should assess the likelihood of impact under four scenarios.

  —Normal operating conditions

  —Start-up and shutdown conditions

  —Abnormal operating conditions

  —Emergency situations

- *Amplitude.* The more extensive the impact, the more significant the aspect.

To the extent allowed by science and technology, the likelihood and amplitude of environmental impacts should be quantified. In the absence of such data, organizations often obtain information from a variety of sources, including scientific journals, regulatory and legislative monitoring, and trade and professional associations.

In concert with the environmental policy, significant environmental aspects and their impacts provide the foundation upon which the EMS is built.

4.3.2 Legal and Other Requirements

> The organization shall establish and maintain a procedure to identify and have access to legal and other requirements to which the organization subscribes, that are applicable to the environmental aspects of its activities, products or services.

A company should have a procedure to identify the legal requirements with which it must comply. It also must have a procedure to provide access to those requirements. Depending on the nature of a company's core operations, this may be highly labor-intensive. Assembling a complete array of federal, state, and local laws and regulations is only the first step in a process that is likely to require periodic updating as changes are enacted.

Such information tends to reside with corporate counsel or corporate environmental health and safety (EHS) staff. Thorough assessment will consider which legal requirements affect specific operations and ascertain whether appropriate personnel are familiar with and have immediate access to every such requirement.

Inland Steel Company, in East Chicago, Indiana, has an effective procedure to ensure ongoing review and dissemination of relevant environmental regulations.[1] A flowchart documents the process.

- The regulations manager, EH&S, reads the table of contents for possible applicable proposed or final regulations in the Federal Register and the Indiana Register.

- The regulations manager reads the summary section of possible applicable regulations to determine whether Inland might be affected.

- Applicable notices are routed to the appropriate responsible engineers. Individual engineers are assigned responsibility for more than a dozen specific environmental issues, such as hazardous materials shipping, RCRA, water, air, and oil spills.

- The engineer reads the notice and contacts appropriate operating departments for input.

- The operating department determines specific effects and supplies needed data to the engineer.

- The engineer prepares a response for the regulations manager.

- For a proposed regulation, the engineer and regulations manager develop a plan for providing comments to the agency. For a final regulation, they develop a regulatory impact flowchart that depicts actions to be taken and deadlines that must be met by various business units and individuals.

Similar procedures must be established for voluntary initiatives to which the company subscribes. Frequently, a company's senior management signs on to such initiatives without communicating to employees how they will be affected by conformance requirements. The voluntary nature of such efforts may lull decision makers into a sense of complacency. However, ISO 14001 requires that such obligations be treated with the same commitment as legal requirements.

4.3.3 Objectives and Targets

> The organization shall establish and maintain documented environmental objectives and targets, at each relevant function and level within the organization.
>
> When establishing and reviewing its objectives, an organization shall consider the legal and other requirements, its significant environmental aspects, its technological options and its financial, operational and business requirements, and the views of interested parties.
>
> The objectives and targets shall be consistent with the environmental policy, including the commitment to prevention of pollution.

The environmental policy and environmental aspects are the foundation upon which the EMS is built. These elements provide guidance for establishing objectives and targets which, in turn, guide all subsequent EMS activities.

Before assessing the degree to which the company's objectives and targets conform to the requirements of ISO 14001, the distinction between these terms and their relationship to the environmental policy should be clarified. The *environmental policy* is a macrolevel statement of an organization's intentions and principles vis-à-vis its overall environmental performance. An example of a policy statement is "conserve natural resources." *Environmental objectives* are overall environmental goals. Examples of objectives that reflect the policy to conserve natural resources are "reduce paper use" and "reduce energy use." *Environmental targets* are detailed performance requirements that must be met to achieve environmental objectives. One example of a target that fulfills the objective of reducing paper use is "reduce paper by 15 percent over previous year's use."

Companies are divided about the degree of difficulty that accompanies targets. Some believe that targets should be stretch targets; that is, they should require considerable effort to achieve. In their view, falling short is not viewed as failure. Others, fearing that failure to achieve a stretch target will be interpreted by third-party auditors as failure to fulfill this requirement and section 4.3.4 of the standard, suggest that targets should be attainable.

Some companies have developed both. They have targets that must be met (such as 35 percent reduction in emission X) and targets that would be highly desirable but unlikely (such as 50 percent reduction in emission X).

In making decisions about target achievability, companies should be guided by the ISO 14001 requirement that objectives and targets reflect the environmental policy and the organization's significant environmental aspects. Assessment, therefore, should not focus merely on the existence of documented objectives and targets. It is important to ascertain whether they contribute to continual improvement, prevention of pollution, and other commitments embodied in the environmental policy and/or identified as significant environmental aspects.

Objectives and targets also should be subjected to a reality check. They should reflect the constraints of current technology, capital, and available skills.

4.3.4 Environmental Management Programme(s)

The organization shall establish and maintain (a) programme(s) for achieving its objectives and targets. It shall include

a) designation of responsibility for achieving objectives and targets at each relevant function and level of the organization;

b) the means and time-frame by which they are to be achieved.

If a project relates to new developments and new or modified activities, products or services, programme(s) shall be amended where relevant to ensure that environmental management applies to such projects.

The environmental management program is directly tied to objectives and targets. It encompasses the planning and logistics that enable an organization to achieve the targets that it has set for itself.

Some companies will integrate the environmental management program with other planning efforts, such as strategic planning. Others will find it easier to maintain the environmental management program as a separate initiative.

Whether an integrated or independent approach is used, an effective program will address critical activities designed to achieve objectives and targets, departmental and individual responsibility for the implementation of those activities, resources, timing, and milestones. The program also should identify the measures that will be used to track progress in achieving established targets.

Clause 4.4, Implementation and Operation

This section of ISO 14001 corresponds to the second step in the Shewhart cycle, do, which involves carrying out actions that were identified during the planning stage. ISO 14001 contains seven elements: structure and responsibility; training, awareness, and competence; communication; EMS documentation; document control; operational control; and emergency preparedness and response. Readers familiar with ISO 9000 will find a number of similarities between the two standards.

4.4.1 Structure and Responsibility

Roles, responsibility and authorities shall be defined, documented and communicated in order to facilitate effective environmental management.

Management shall provide resources essential to the implementation and control of the environmental management system. Resources include human resources and specialized skills, technology and financial resources.

The organization's top management shall appoint (a) specific management representative(s) who, irrespective of other responsibilities, shall have defined roles, responsibilities and authority for

a) ensuring that environmental management system requirements are established, implemented and maintained in accordance with this International Standard;

b) reporting on the performance of the environmental management system to top management for review and as a basis for improvement of the environmental management system.

The distinction between responsibility and authority is important for understanding the intended purpose of this element. Within the context of an EMS, responsibility pertains to specific tasks or obligations with which one is charged; authority pertains to influence and power.

Individuals with responsibility do not necessarily have authority. The environmental manager within a facility may have the responsibility for establishing an environmental awareness training program, yet lack the authority to require attendance by plant employees who report to an operations manager.

ISO 14001 attempts to ensure that a chief environmental officer—the "other" CEO—has the power to guarantee that assigned responsibilities are accomplished and needed resources are available to fulfill ISO 14001 requirements.

4.4.2 Training, Awareness and Competence

The organization shall identify training needs. It shall require that all personnel whose work may create a significant impact upon the environment, have received appropriate training.

It shall establish and maintain procedures to make its employees or members at each relevant function and level aware of

a) the importance of conformance with the environmental policy and procedures and with the requirements of the environmental management system;

b) the significant environmental impacts, actual or potential, of their work activities and the environmental benefits of improved personal performance;

c) their roles and responsibilities in achieving conformance with the environmental policy and procedures and with the requirements of the environmental management system, including emergency preparedness and response requirements;

d) the potential consequences of departure from specified operating procedures.

> Personnel performing the tasks which can cause significant environmental impacts shall be competent on the basis of appropriate education, training and/or experience.

This element addresses two areas of training: skills or competence training for employees whose work may have a significant environmental impact, and general awareness training for employees throughout the organization.

Personnel whose work can cause significant environmental impacts must be competent to perform those tasks. Competence—defined as the effective execution of required actions—can be attained through avenues other than training, such as formal education and/or experience. It is incumbent upon company management to define competence and identify training needs for those employees whose on-the-job performance does not meet defined competence levels.

It quickly becomes apparent that identification of training needs is directly related to identification of a company's environmental aspects and their significant environmental impacts (section 4.3.1). Therefore, training needs are likely to go beyond those courses that are mandated by regulation.

A forest products company with a strong commitment to environmental stewardship established a formal environmental training department in 1993. Previously it had conducted periodic training programs on topics of special interest or emerging importance, but with the increasing number of environmental laws and regulations, it recognized the need to develop a comprehensive training program. In 1995, it offered the following courses.

- General courses
    - Introduction to environmental regulations
    - Environmental management
- Air courses
    - Prevention of significant deterioration permitting/applicability
    - Title V permitting and operational issues
    - Source monitoring
    - Emission estimating techniques

—Boiler operations—environmental concerns

—Air pollution meteorology/dispersion modeling

—Air pollution control—principles of design and operation

• Water courses

—Stormwater pollution prevention plans and practices

—Introduction to wastewater basics

—Principles of wastewater treatment systems for pulp and paper

—Wastewater treatment system modeling for pulp and paper

—Laboratory quality assurance/quality control procedures

—Groundwater fundamentals/monitoring

• Solid waste courses

—Nonhazardous waste

—Hazardous waste

• Other courses

—Superfund Amendments and Reauthorization Act

—Spills and releases—spill prevention control and counter-measures

—Wetlands orientation

Although the standard does not explicitly mention on-site contractors or temporary employees, management should be cognizant of the specific activities in which such individuals are involved. If those activities could result in significant environmental impact, management should consider whether to require the same level of competence and accountability that it demands of its own employees. This does not place the burden of training on the contracting organization. As a condition of doing business, a company can require that contractors provide evidence of appropriate experience and training for all on-site contractors.

General awareness training is intended to emphasize the importance of conforming to ISO 14001 and reinforce the environmental benefits of improved individual performance. Therefore, it should be offered to a broad array of employees. In addition to operators and line managers, awareness training should be available to employees at all levels, from senior management down to the most junior individuals in the organization. It also should include employees from both production-related and nonproduction-related business units such as finance, marketing, sales, and procurement.

The company's environmental awareness training program has been designed to fulfill the following objectives.

- Make all employees aware of the company's commitment to be the environmental leader in its industry.

- Create awareness of each employee's individual environmental responsibility.

- Create a behavior change that will improve employees environmental performance.

The program finds audiences throughout the company. Participants in the program include top management; group, area, and manufacturing managers; facility managers; supervisors; environmental staff; hourly employees; and union employees. To ensure utility, the program focuses on business unit–specific and facility-specific environmental issues.

All training must be documented. Although section 4.4.2 does not indicate this requirement, section 4.5.3, Records, specifies that procedures for the identification, maintenance, and disposition of records, including training records, must be established.

4.4.3 Communication

With regard to its environmental aspects and environmental management system, the organization shall establish and maintain procedures for

a) internal communication between the various levels and functions of the organization;

b) receiving, documenting and responding to relevant communication from external interested parties.

The organization shall consider processes for external communication on its significant environmental aspects and record its decision.

U.S. companies tend to have far-reaching communication mechanisms that cascade information down through the organization. Less pervasive are procedures for encouraging communication across functional areas and from lower levels up to higher levels in the organization. As used here, the phrase "relevant function and level" refers to multidirectional internal communication procedures that enable access to relevant information.

ISO 14001 differs markedly from other EMS standards in the area of external communication. Unlike the European EMAS, which requires an annual environmental performance statement, and BS 7750, which requires that the environmental policy indicate how environmental objectives will be made publicly available, ISO 14001 does not require public disclosure of any environmental information other than the environmental policy. The only communication requirement applicable to external parties is reactive in nature: Companies must document and respond to relevant communication.

4.4.4 Environmental Management System Documentation

> The organization shall establish and maintain information, in paper or electronic form, to
>
> a) describe the core elements of the management system and their interaction;
>
> b) provide direction to related documentation.

Documentation of the EMS can take any form that is useful to a company. ISO 14001 does not require a single manual, nor does it dictate the kinds of information that should be maintained.

Companies are likely to find that the ISO 9000 documentation model is easily adaptable to fulfill the requirements of this element. Companies that have, or plan to obtain, ISO 9000 certification will benefit from the ability to easily integrate the two sets of documentation. EMS documentation based on the ISO 9000 model will encompass three levels.

1. An EMS manual. This is an umbrella document that provides an overview of the EMS and describes how each ISO 14001 element is being achieved.

2. EMS procedures. At a minimum, this should include all procedures specified in ISO 14001 (for example, the procedure to identify environmental aspects). Such procedures tend to be interdepartmental; that is, they are applicable across the company's functions and levels.

3. Environmental records, reports, forms, and other similar accounts and measures of environmental performance.

Some companies may elect to expand their documentation by including work instructions. These detailed explanations of how specific tasks are to be carried out should reflect the company's environmental aspects and regulatory requirements.

4.4.5 Document Control

The organization shall establish and maintain procedures for controlling all documents required by this International Standard to ensure that

a) they can be located;

b) they are periodically reviewed, revised as necessary and approved for adequacy by authorized personnel;

c) the current versions of relevant documents are available at all locations where operations essential to the effective functioning of the environmental management system are performed;

d) obsolete documents are promptly removed from all points of issue and points of use or otherwise assured against unintended use;

e) any obsolete documents retained for legal and/or knowledge preservation purposes are suitably identified.

Documentation shall be legible, dated (with dates of revision), and readily identifiable, maintained in an orderly manner and retained for a specified period. Procedures and responsibilities shall be established and maintained concerning the creation and modification of the various types of document.

According to Annex A, the purpose of this requirement is to ensure that organizations create and maintain documents in a manner sufficient to implement the EMS. The obvious question, then, is "How much is sufficient?"

ISO 14001 distinguishes between documented procedures and procedures. Only three procedures must be documented.

1. Operating procedures for activities associated with significant environmental aspects (4.4.6a)

2. Monitoring and measurement of activities that can have a significant environmental impact (4.5.1)

3. Periodic evaluation of regulatory compliance (4.5.1)

In addition, 11 activities must be documented.

1. Environmental policy (section 4.2e)

2. Environmental objectives (4.3.3)

3. Roles, responsibilities, and authorities (4.4.1)

4. Communication from external parties (4.4.3b)

5. Decision regarding external communication about significant environmental aspects (4.4.3)

6. EMS documentation (4.4.4)

7. Calibration and maintenance of monitoring equipment (4.5.1)

8. Changes in any documented procedures (4.5.2)

9. Training (4.5.3)

10. Results of audits and reviews (4.5.3)

11. Management review of the EMS (4.6)

Another 10 elements require that the organization establish and maintain procedures without requiring that such procedures be documented. These 11 procedures are as follows:

1. Identification of environmental aspects (4.3.1)

2. Identification of and access to legal and other requirements (4.3.2)

3. Identification of training needs (4.4.2)

4. Internal communication (4.4.3)

5. Receiving, documenting, and responding to relevant communication from external interested parties (4.4.3)

6. Document control (4.4.5)

7. Identifiable significant environmental aspects of goods and services used by the organization (4.4.6c)

8. Identification of the potential for and response to accidents and emergencies (4.4.7)

9. Defining responsibility and authority for addressing nonconformance and corrective/preventive action (4.5.2)

10. Identification, maintenance, and disposition of environmental records (4.5.3)

11. EMS audits (4.5.4)

Some companies will demonstrate the existence and implementation of these procedures through means other than formal documentation. For example, personal observation coupled with employee interviews that elicit consistent, clear descriptions about specific procedures is one means of verifying that required procedures are in place despite the absence of written documentation. Many companies, however, are choosing to document these 11 procedures. Formal documentation minimizes the risk of departure from established practices, simplifies training, and facilitates internal audits and management review of the EMS.

Companies must decide whether formal documentation of these elements adds value to the organization's efforts to implement, maintain, and review the EMS. Companies with ISO 9000 quality systems also should determine whether integration of selected elements makes more sense than creating separate, duplicative procedures. The ISO 9000 procedure for handling records, for example, may adequately fulfill the ISO 14001 requirement. (See section III for areas of overlap between ISO 9001 and ISO 14001.)

Whether a company limits itself to the mandated documented procedures or creates additional documents, it must establish a procedure for managing those documents. This is an instance in which less may be more. Annex A clearly states that the organization's primary focus should be the effective implementation of its EMS, not a complex documentation control system.

Ultimately, all documentation should be clear, usable, and informative. If it is not understandable, either by those within the organization or external auditors, it is not useful.

ISO 14001 allows flexibility in this area. Documentation can appear on paper or in electronic databases. Flowcharts may supplement or replace text. In some circumstances, videotaped demonstrations may be superior to written instructions. Companies should use whatever mechanisms and formats contribute most effectively to the utility of the document in question.

4.4.6 Operational Control

The organization shall identify those operations and activities that are associated with the identified significant environmental aspects in line with its policy, objectives and targets. The organization shall plan these activities, including maintenance, in order to ensure that they are carried out under specified conditions by

a) establishing and maintaining documented procedures to cover situations where their absence could lead to deviations from the environmental policy and the objectives and targets;

b) stipulating operating criteria in the procedures;

c) establishing and maintaining procedures related to the identifiable significant environmental aspects of goods and services used by the organization and communicating relevant procedures and requirements to suppliers and contractors.

The majority of U.S. companies have documented operating procedures and work instructions for every facet of their operations. Many of these procedures and instructions implicitly address environmental concerns.

ISO 14001 does not require documented procedures for every activity associated with significant environmental aspects. It requires such procedures for those activities where the lack of a procedure could result in a failure to adequately address established environmental priorities.

4.4.7 Emergency Preparedness and Response

> The organization shall establish and maintain procedures to identify potential for and respond to accidents and emergency situations, and for preventing and mitigating the environmental impacts that may be associated with them.
>
> The organization shall review and revise, where necessary, its emergency preparedness and response procedures, in particular, after the occurrence of accidents or emergency situations.
>
> The organization shall also periodically test such procedures where practicable.

The purpose of this requirement is to ensure that companies will respond appropriately when faced with an accident or other unexpected incident. Because a comprehensive assessment of environmental aspects addresses the likelihood of environmental impact under abnormal operating conditions and emergency situations, many companies find it practical to link that procedure with this requirement. The emergency plans that are legally required in many U.S. companies generally are adequate to fulfill this requirement.

Clause 4.5, Checking and Corrective Action

This component of ISO 14001 corresponds to the check stage of the Shewhart cycle. The standard contains four elements that are intended to measure and evaluate the effects of actions taken during implementation and operation: monitoring and measurement; nonconformance and corrective and preventive action; records; and the EMS audit.

4.5.1 Monitoring and Measurement

> The organization shall establish and maintain documented procedures to monitor and measure, on a regular basis, the key characteristics of its operations and

activities that can have a significant impact on the environment. This shall include the recording of information to track performance, relevant operational controls and conformance with the organization's objectives and targets.

Monitoring equipment shall be calibrated and maintained and records of this process shall be retained according to the organization's procedures.

The organization shall establish and maintain a documented procedure for periodically evaluating compliance with relevant environmental legislation and regulations.

Although ISO 14001 is not an environmental performance standard, it requires that companies compare their actual environmental performance with the performance levels designated by objectives and targets. Such comparisons are intended to determine whether the organization is achieving the goals embodied in its environmental policy and addressed through its environmental management program.

Although specific performance measures will reflect critical environmental aspects of a company's activities and, therefore, are likely to differ from one organization to another, all performance measures should be characterized by the following:

- *Access*—Data should be readily obtainable.

- *Adequacy*—Data should be appropriate for their intended use.

- *Validity*—Data should measure what they are intended to measure.

- *Reliability*—Data are accurate. This is addressed, in part, by the requirement that monitoring equipment is calibrated and maintained.

There also must be a documented procedure to determine whether the company is in compliance with its legal requirements. For some U.S. companies, this takes the form of the compliance audit. Others rely on the monitoring data mandated by various operating permits.

4.5.2 Nonconformance and Corrective and Preventive Action

> The organization shall establish and maintain procedures for defining responsibility and authority for handling and investigating nonconformance, taking action to mitigate any impacts caused and for initiating and completing corrective and preventive action.
>
> Any corrective or preventive action taken to eliminate the causes of actual and potential nonconformances shall be appropriate to the magnitude of problems and commensurate with the environmental impact encountered.
>
> The organization shall implement and record any changes in the documented procedures resulting from corrective and preventive action.

This element pertains to any failure to fulfill a requirement of ISO 14001. It does not refer to regulatory noncompliance, although it frequently is misinterpreted as such. This suggests that regulatory noncompliance is addressed only to the extent that procedures for identifying legal requirements or periodically evaluating compliance with applicable legal requirements have not been established or appropriately maintained.

In practice, an EMS audit will seek to identify nonconformities with any requirement of ISO 14001. Therefore, nonconformances that are identified in conjunction with any assessment, audit, or other review of the EMS are subject to the procedures established here. Annex A of ISO 14001 states that in establishing and maintaining procedures for "investigating and correcting nonconformance," the cause should be identified, corrective action should be identified and implemented, controls should be implemented or modified to avoid repetition, and any changes in written procedures resulting from the corrective action should be recorded.

4.5.3 Records

> The organization shall establish and maintain procedures for the identification, maintenance and disposition of environmental records. These records shall

include training records and the results of audits and reviews.

Environmental records shall be legible, identifiable and traceable to the activity, product or service involved. Environmental records shall be stored and maintained in such a way that they are readily retrievable and protected against damage, deterioration or loss. Their retention times shall be established and recorded.

Records shall be maintained, as appropriate to the system and to the organization, to demonstrate conformance to the requirements of this International Standard.

Most organizations find that developing procedures to identify, maintain, and dispose of records is relatively straightforward. Less easily accomplished is deciding what kinds of records should be retained.

At a minimum, information required by regulation (such as material safety data sheets) should be included. Annex A suggests the following:

- Legislative and regulatory requirements
- Training records
- Process information
- Product information
- Inspection, maintenance, and calibration records
- Incident reports
- Information on significant environmental aspects
- Audit results
- Management reviews

Unless required by law, companies are free to determine how long such records will be maintained.

4.5.4 Environmental Management System Audit

The organization shall establish and maintain (a) programme(s) and procedures for periodic environmental management system audits to be carried out, in order to

a) determine whether or not the environmental management system

  1) conforms to planned arrangements for environmental management, including the requirements of this International Standard; and

  2) has been properly implemented and maintained; and

b) provide information on the results of audits to management.

The organisation's audit programme, including any schedule, shall be based on the environmental importance of the activity concerned and the results of previous audits. In order to be comprehensive, the audit procedures shall cover the audit scope, frequency and methodologies, as well as the responsibilities and requirements for conducting audits and reporting results.

The EMS audit is intended to ensure that the EMS conforms to all requirements of ISO 14001 and that senior managers have a thorough understanding of its strengths and weaknesses. Annex A suggests that the audit program encompass six elements.

1. *Activities and areas to be considered in audits.* The greatest challenge in conducting an EMS audit is a clear understanding of the parameters that bound the activity. An EMS audit is neither a compliance nor a performance audit. Its purpose is to verify that appropriate procedures are in place and functioning to ensure conformance with ISO 14001.

This point is illustrated by evaluation of the requirement in section 4.5.1 that the organization "shall establish and maintain a documented procedure for periodically evaluating compliance with relevant environmental legislation and regulations." The EMS audit does not evaluate compliance with regulatory requirements. It evaluates the *procedure* to evaluate compliance with regulatory requirements. Thus, an EMS audit would

—Evaluate senior management's commitment to regulatory compliance

—Evaluate the implementation of the regulatory compliance procedure

—Determine whether there is a review process that validates or revises the procedure as necessary

2. *Frequency of audits.* The scope and complexity of the EMS will play a key role in determining how often audits are conducted. Smaller entities may elect to audit on an annual basis. Larger, more complex organizations are likely to find that a longer interval between audits is desirable.

ISO 9000 may be instructive in determining the acceptable frequency of EMS audits. ISO 9000 certification requires a full audit every three years and surveillance audits every six months. An ISO 14001 audit program could follow the example established by the quality system audit cycle. Full audits could be conducted every two or three years. Areas of nonconformance would be targeted for surveillance audits at selected intervals, say every six months. For an EMS with no nonconformances, different elements could be addressed during surveillance audits, such that all elements are audited at least once during the interval between full audits.

3. *Responsibilities associated with managing and conducting audits.* Individuals who serve as members of an audit team will find themselves with different responsibilities. For example, the lead auditor might be responsible for assembling the audit team, acting as liaison with senior management of the business unit to be audited, and developing the final audit report. Auditors might be responsible for assisting in the development of checklists and interview protocols that will be used during the audit. Technical experts might provide specialized information about specific regulatory requirements or manufacturing processes that are subject to review during the audit.

ISO 10011-1, *Guidelines for auditing quality systems,* and ISO 14011, *Auditing of environmental management systems,* delineate specific responsibilities of auditors and lead auditors.

4. *Communication of audit findings.* Audit procedures should assign responsibility for communicating audit finds and designate those individuals to whom such findings are to be conveyed. At a minimum, audit findings must be communicated to top management, as required by ISO 14001. However, companies may deem it appropriate to share results with others in the organization.

5. *Auditor competence.* In developing audit procedures, attention must be directed to auditor competence and the qualifications that will be used to determine competence. Organizations tend to define competence in terms of educational attainment and professional experience.

ISO 14012, *Qualification criteria for environmental auditors,* does not explicitly define competence. It implies that competence is ensured by "currency of knowledge" of the following topics.

—Aspects of relevant environmental science and technology

—Appropriate technical and environmental aspects of facility operations

—Relevant environmental laws, regulations, and related documents

—Environmental management systems and related standards

—Auditing processes, procedures, and techniques

ISO 14012 describes auditor qualifications as follows:

—Auditors must have completed at least secondary education or its equivalent.

—Auditors with a secondary education should have a minimum of five years' appropriate work experience.

—Auditors with a college degree should have a minimum of four years' appropriate work experience.

—In addition, auditors should have completed both formal and on-the-job training. Formal training is not explicitly described; however, the standard does state that it should address the five areas delineated under competence.

On-the-job training is defined as a minimum of four environmental audits for a total of 20 workdays. This on-the-job training must occur under the supervision of a lead auditor and must be completed within a three-year period.

—Lead auditors must meet all of the qualifications for auditors. In addition, a lead auditor must participate in three more audits (for a total of seven) that span 15 workdays (for a total of 35). These additional criteria must be met within a three-year period. Alternatively, lead auditors can demonstrate appropriate attributes through interviews, references, or other assessments.

ISO 14012 is intended only as a guideline. Companies are free to establish their own auditor qualifications criteria.

6. *How audits will be conducted.* A key decision here is whether to use internal or external auditors. Internal auditors are likely to have an understanding of the company's legal obligations and operating processes that cannot be matched by external consultants. The risk of conflicts of interest can be minimized by ensuring that internal auditors are independent of the business units that they are auditing.

Conversely, external auditors often are better able to view company activities objectively because they are unfettered by institutional memory. Their exposure to diverse strategies for fulfilling specific requirements of the standard, gained through experience in auditing other companies, may provide a more realistic interpretation of ISO 14001 than occurs with internal auditors.

The audit approach currently in favor entails a combination of internal and external auditors. This tactic allows the company to capitalize on the strengths offered by both groups of auditors.

Clause 4.6, Management Review

The final component of ISO 14001 parallels the final stage of the Shewhart cycle, act.

> The organization's top management shall, at intervals that it determines, review the environmental management system, to ensure its continuing suitability, adequacy and effectiveness. The management review process shall ensure that the necessary information is collected to allow management to carry out this evaluation. This review shall be documented.

> The management review shall address the possible need for changes to policy, objectives and elements of the environmental management system, in the light of environmental management system audit results, changing circumstances and the commitment to continual improvement.

ISO 14001 defines continual improvement as a process of "enhancing the EMS to achieve improvements in overall environmental performance in line with the organization's environmental policy." The purpose of management review is to identify opportunities for improving the EMS.

Senior management should examine the extent to which objectives and targets reflect the environmental policy and significant environmental aspects and impacts and have been met. Additionally, management should consider whether changes in legislation, organizational activities, technology, or concerns of external interested parties dictates any changes in the EMS.

Information obtained through communication strategies (4.4.3), monitoring and measurement (4.5.1), corrective action (4.5.2), and results of EMS audits (4.5.4) may be of particular value in determining where improvements can be realized.

Note

1. Interviews with Inland Steel Company EH&S staff, November 1995.

Chapter 6

Assessing an Existing Environmental Management System

Assessing an environmental management system is commonly referred to as *gap analysis*. Gap analysis entails exactly what the name suggests—comparing a company's existing environmental policies, procedures, and practices to the requirements imposed by ISO 14001 to determine where discrepancies exist. The results of gap analysis can be used by company management to determine the actions that are required to correct identified deficiencies, the cost of such actions, and the amount of time needed to achieve the desired results.

Gap analysis can be performed with both *qualitative* and *quantitative* data. Although these terms have precise definitions among statisticians, ISO 14001 assigns them less rigorous meanings. Within the context of the standard, qualitative data involve attribute or kind. A qualitative chemical analysis, for example, would identify the components of a substance or mixture. Quantitative data involve the measurement of amount. Using the same example, a quantitative chemical analysis would determine the amounts of the components of a substance.

Regardless of its type, all data employed in gap analysis must be objective. That is, it must be expressed in terms that are unbiased by personal feelings or interpretations.

Like many companies, H.B. Fuller Company initiated its consideration of ISO 14001 with a gap analysis.

H.B. Fuller Company

H.B. Fuller Company was founded in 1887 as a manufacturer of wall-paper paste. Today, Fuller is a worldwide formulator, manufacturer, and marketer of adhesives, sealants, coatings, paints, and other specialty chemical products. Manufacturing and sales operations employ 6400 people in 43 countries.

The company's largest worldwide business category is adhesives, sealants, and coatings. These products, in thousands of formulations, are sold to customers in a wide range of industries, including packaging, woodworking, automotive, aerospace, graphic arts (books/magazines), appliances, windows, sporting goods, nonwovens, shoes, and ceramic tile.

Fuller is also a quality producer and supplier of powder coatings to metal finishing industries; commercial and industrial paints in Latin American markets; specialty waxes in European markets; mastics and coatings for thermal insulation, for improving indoor air quality, and asbestos abatement applications; and sanitation chemicals to the dairy, beverage, and food processing industries.

Fuller's Environmental Commitment

Fuller has a proud history of proactive community involvement. The company's mission statement expresses responsibility, including environmental leadership and social responsibility, to customers, employees, shareholders, and communities (in ranked order). According to Anthony L. Andersen, chairman of the board, Fuller's attention to environmental concerns is philosophically rooted in the belief that it's the right thing to do.

In 1986, Fuller's board of directors established the Worldwide Environment, Health, and Safety (WEHS) committee. Representatives from Fuller's four geographic regions—Asia/Pacific, Europe, Latin America, and North America—meet annually with corporate staffs to discuss existing and emerging environmental issues and develop appropriate standards or programs for implementation.

That same year, Fuller also created the WEHS Oversight Committee, which is chaired by its chairman of the board. The company's president and CEO, senior vice presidents, and vice presidents also participate on the six-member committee. The Oversight Committee reviews and approves all WEHS committee recommendations regarding policies, standards, programs, and other actions.

In 1993, Fuller affirmed the CERES Principles. *FORTUNE* magazine identified the company as one of "The 10 Environmental Leaders."[1] And Fuller published its first EHS progress report during the year.

WEHS Policy Statement

H.B. Fuller Company will implement environmental, health and safety programs that will be, at a minimum, in compliance with local regulations. The programs will be consistent with standard worldwide requirements established and maintained by the Worldwide Environment, Health and Safety Committee. Special considerations will be given to the specific hazards at each operation and potential employee and neighborhood exposures. We will strive to prevent the release of any pollutant that may cause adverse effects to the environment. We will minimize the creation of waste, especially hazardous waste. We will reduce, and where possible eliminate, the environmental, health and safety risks to our employees and the communities in which we operate. All managers/supervisors shall ensure compliance with this policy within their area of responsibility.

In 1995, Fuller decided to assess its existing EMS in comparison to ISO 14001 (referred to hereafter as *gap analysis*). This action was recommended by the corporate EHS department, endorsed by the WEHS committee, and approved by the WEHS Oversight Committee. Fuller believes that it makes sense to pool all environmental management programs under a single umbrella with worldwide applicability.

Customer demand was not a factor in Fuller's decision to consider adoption of ISO 14001. However, company managers acknowledge that in the next few years, multinational customers, like the Big Three automobile manufacturers, might require that their suppliers demonstrate conformity to an EMS standard. The ISO 14000 series standards have the greatest international acceptance as a global standard.

Fuller's approach to gap analysis, described in detail by the corporate EHS department, began with an internal communication effort targeted toward three important groups: worldwide area coordinators, corporate EHS staff, and ISO 9000 staff.

• In May, 1995, Fuller introduced the ISO 14000 series standards to its worldwide area coordinators in conjunction with their annual meeting. The purpose of that session was to describe the objective and requirements of ISO 14001 and its likely impact on the company's stakeholders (for example, customers and regulators) and, therefore, its potential impact on Fuller.

• In June 1995, the information presented at the May meeting was sent to the WEHS Oversight Committee as a "heads up."

• A second special training session for WEHS Area Coordinators was held in October 1995. It focused on ISO 14001 (EMS specification) and ISO 14010 (auditing principles).

• Corporate EHS staff also engage in a monthly dialogue with the company's ISO 9000 staff. (Nine Fuller facilities have obtained ISO 9000 certification and another five or more will be audited for certification during 1996.) EHS staff believe that ISO 14001 will be easier to implement by adapting existing quality procedures in areas of overlap with EMS requirements, such as document control and records.

Once the Oversight Committee has adopted conformance with the ISO 14001 standard, Fuller will expand its communication effort to include employees throughout the organization. *Fuller World*, a quarterly newsletter that is mailed to every employee's home address, will be used to disseminate the Oversight Committee's position, other articles about ISO 14001 in general, or the gap analysis effort.

Fuller's approach to conducting gap analysis entails internal examination of corporate environmental programs and activities. Corporate EHS staff are looking at all existing environmental guidelines, programs, and procedures, comparing Fuller's initiatives to the ISO 14001 requirements, and identifying what changes are necessary to fully conform to the requirements of the standard.

The corporate EHS department estimates that completion of this process will require approximately one year. Several decisions influenced this timeline.

• Gap analysis is performed only by corporate EHS staff. No external consultants have been involved in the process and none are anticipated.

- Gap analysis is performed on a part-time basis. Corporate EHS staff are conducting the comparison in addition to their other job responsibilities.

- Productivity and product quality cannot be compromised. Fuller's decision to perform gap analysis activities in a manner that interferes only minimally with business objectives lengthens the time required to obtain needed information.

Interim Gap Analysis Findings

As Fuller reached the midpoint in its gap analysis effort, interim findings revealed several issues that could impede successful implementation of ISO 14001. None of these issues is insurmountable, and Fuller has taken steps to resolve them. They are presented here because they illustrate the kinds of impediments that, if not recognized and addressed, can derail successful implementation of an EMS.

- *Implicit versus explicit intent.* Fuller discovered that ISO 14001 requires explicit articulation of desired outcomes. Fuller's WEHS policy, for example, needs to specify the company's commitment to continual improvement, although it can be inferred. The policy also needs to correlate Fuller's commitment to the CERES Principles, as required by other requirements in section 4.2c.

- *R&D "creativity" versus EHS limitations.* EHS views identification of environmental aspects and impacts as a proactive, preventive initiative; R&D views the same procedure as a hindrance to creativity. Fuller acknowledges that better communication with its R&D group is necessary to develop and foster acceptance of a balanced approach that encourages creativity yet integrates with proper engineering safeguards.

- *Performance criteria and comparisons.* Although Fuller has established measures for its environmental objectives and targets, gap analysis suggested that additional performance measurement criteria for demonstrating continual improvement should be established. Fuller also determined that an integrated database management system would enable the company to analyze trends across media, something that its existing system cannot do easily or comprehensively.

• *Corporate versus area and facility responsibilities.* Clear delineation of corporate, area, and facility environmental responsibility and authority concerning nonconformance and preventive and corrective action was not always apparent. Depending on the specific issue of concern, follow-up action was delayed because the responsible party assumed a different group was accountable, or duplicative actions were taken because more than one group believed that it was to resolve the problem.

The single greatest nonconformity concerned documentation of procedures. Fuller discovered that further documentation of activities will be required by ISO 14001, even though company practice frequently fulfilled the intended purpose of the standard.

Conclusion

Although Fuller will not make a decision about implementing ISO 14001 until it has completed the gap analysis, early indications suggest a strong likelihood that ISO 14001 will be adopted.

Conducting Gap Analysis

With proper planning, gap analysis is a straightforward process that focuses on the specific requirements of a standard (in this case, ISO 14001) and concomitant company actions that might contribute to fulfillment of those requirements. Effective gap analysis is based on three related sets of information.

1. Specific requirements with which a company must conform. For example, *Top management shall define the organization's environmental policy.*

2. Questions that determine whether a company is operating in a manner that appropriately meets specific requirements. For example, *Who developed the organization's policy?*

3. Sources of objective data that provide answers to questions. For example, *interviews with senior managers, minutes of management committee meetings.*

U.S. companies are likely to find that many of the ISO 14001 elements are addressed to some extent as a result of regulatory requirements. The most common nonconformances are found in the areas of communication and documentation. Although many companies have accepted practices and procedures, these often are not formally documented and distributed to all affected employees.

The challenge for companies that conduct gap analysis is focusing on the EMS itself rather than environmental performance. Two elements where many companies experience particular difficulty are environmental aspects and monitoring and measurement. From an assessment standpoint, it is necessary to focus on procedures to identify the environmental aspects of a company's activities, products, or services rather than the actual aspects themselves. Similarly, gap analysis related to evaluation of environmental impacts should focus on the procedures and practices that are in place, rather than the actual or potential impacts.

The requirement to establish a procedure for periodic evaluation of regulatory compliance poses a similar challenge. Gap analysis should not involve a compliance audit. Rather, it must determine whether an organization has a procedure for discovering regulatory violations.

The remainder of this section contains a series of Figures 6.1–6.17, that delineate the specific requirements of each ISO 14001 element, questions that can elicit the information necessary to assess the elements, and data sources for the objective evidence that is demanded by an auditor. Questions and data sources are illustrative, not exhaustive. The reader is encouraged to modify these lists to make them more useful.

Note

1. Faye Rice, "Who Scores Best on the Environment," *FORTUNE*, 26 July 1995, 114–122.

ISO 14001 requirements	Questions	Data sources
Top management shall define the policy.	Who developed the company's environmental policy?	Procedures/practices for developing company policies; records of review/revision of the policy; interviews with individuals familiar with the policy development process.
The policy must be a) Appropriate to the company's environmental impacts b) Committed to continual improvement c) Committed to prevention of pollution d) Committed to regulatory compliance e) Committed to compliance with other requirements to which the company subscribes	Does the policy mention • Continual improvement? • Prevention of pollution? • Compliance with relevant legislation and regulations? • Commitment to voluntary standards or codes of practice? Which ones?	Policy statement, mission statement, environmental manual, annual report, internal and external speeches, published interviews.
f) Documented, implemented, and maintained	Is the policy documented? How?	Policy statement, environmental manual, annual report.
The policy must be g) Communicated to all employees	How has the policy been communicated internally?	Internal newsletters, awareness programs, bulletin boards, speeches, audiotapes/videotapes, teleconferencing.
	Do employees throughout the company understand the policy?	Interviews with employees.
	Do employees throughout the company comply with the policy?	Objectives and targets, job descriptions, performance requirements, audit findings, work procedures.

Figure 6.1. 4.2, environmental policy gap analysis.

ISO 14001 requirements	Questions	Data sources
	How does management ensure continued adherence to the policy?	Environmental planning documents, work procedures, performance reviews.
h) Available to the public	How has the policy been communicated externally?	Press releases, annual report, awareness programs, public announcements, town meetings, TV/radio spots, newspaper articles, speeches, interviews with individuals responsible for company communications.

Figure 6.1. *continued.*

ISO 14001 requirements	Questions	Data sources
Procedure to identify the environmental aspects that the company can control or influence. Determination of significant environmental impacts. Aspects with significant impacts shall be considered in setting environmental objectives and targets. This information shall be kept up-to-date.	How are environmental aspects identified for • Operating activities? • Products? • Services? Are the environmental aspects of normal operating conditions routinely examined and clearly understood throughout the company? Are the environmental aspects of purchased products and services routinely examined and clearly understood throughout the company?	Documented procedures. Demonstrated practices. Interviews with individuals responsible for developing and implementing procedures and/or practices. Interviews comparing actual practice with stated procedures. Records related to design, implementation, and application of procedures/practices. Checklists.

Figure 6.2. 4.3.1, environmental aspects gap analysis.

ISO 14001 requirements	Questions	Data sources
Determination of significant environmental impacts. Aspects with significant impacts shall be considered in setting environmental objectives and targets. This information shall be up-to-date.	Are the environmental aspects of potential abnormal operating conditions routinely examined and clearly understood throughout the company? Have potentially serious or irreversible environmental impacts of past activities been identified? Have potentially serious or irreversible environmental impacts of current activities been identified? Are potentially serious or irreversible environmental impacts of planned activities identified prior to implementation? How broadly are above impacts evaluated (for example, locally, regionally, globally)? How are significant aspects reflected in objectives and targets? How often are aspects/ impacts reviewed?	Direct inspection and measurement. Process flowcharting. Results of previous audits or reviews. Literature reviews and technical articles. Documented procedures. Demonstrated practices. Interviews with individuals responsible for developing and implementing procedures and/or practices. Interviews comparing actual practice with stated procedures. Checklists. Direct inspection and measurement. Results of previous audits or reviews. Documented objectives and targets. Procedures, practices, interviews.

Figure 6.2. *continued.*

ISO 14001 requirements	Questions	Data sources
Procedure to identify legal requirements. Procedure to have access to legal requirements. Procedure to identify other requirements to which the company subscribes that are directly applicable to its environmental aspects. Procedure to have access to other requirements.	With what legal and regulatory requirements must the company comply? How are such requirements identified? Updated? By whom? How and to whom are legal requirements communicated? Does the company subscribe to any voluntary standards or codes of practice concerning the environment? How and to whom are voluntary standards/codes of practice communicated? How does the company ensure that its activities conform to voluntary standards and codes of practice?	Documented procedure. Demonstrated practice. Interviews with individuals responsible for developing and implementing the procedures and practices. Formal communication methods. Compliance records (such as audit reports, permit monitoring requirements). Progress reports regarding voluntary requirements. Interviews with employees concerning understanding of and adherence to legal and voluntary requirements.

Figure 6.3. 4.3.2, legal and other requirements gap analysis.

ISO 14001 requirements	Questions	Data sources
Documented environmental objectives. Documented targets. Consideration of • Legal and other requirements • Significant environmental aspects • Technological options • Financial, operational, business requirements • Views of interested parties Consistency with environmental policy.	For which functions and levels have environmental objectives been established? Are objectives accompanied by specific targets? Do objectives and targets reflect • The views of interested parties? • Significant environmental aspects and impacts? Are objectives and targets consistent with • The environmental policy? • Prevention of pollution? • Continual improvement? How are objectives and targets evaluated? Updated?	Documented objectives. Measurable targets for each objective. Internal memoranda. Minutes of management and staff meetings. Job descriptions. Employee performance requirements. Designation of formal responsibility and accountability.

Figure 6.4. 4.3.3, objectives and targets gap analysis.

ISO 14001 requirements	Questions	Data sources
Program for achieving objectives and targets. Designation of responsibility for achieving objectives and targets. The means for achieving objectives and targets. The time frame for achieving objectives and targets. Application of program to new or modified activities, products, or services.	Who is responsible for achieving objectives and targets? Is there a method for achieving objectives and targets? What? Has a time frame for achievement been determined? What is it? How is progress toward achievement measured? By whom?	Organization charts. Strategic/business plans. Activity schedules. Job descriptions. Interviews to determine whether actual work matches job descriptions.

Figure 6.5. 4.3.4, environmental management program(s) gap analysis.

ISO 14001 requirements	Questions	Data sources
Definition, documentation, and communication of roles, responsibilities, and authorities. Provision of resources essential to the EMS, including • Human resources and specialized skills • Technology • Financial resources Appointed management representative to • Ensure that EMS conforms to ISO 14001 • Report on EMS performance to top management	Does the company have a specific individual with authority for ensuring conformance to ISO 14001? Who? Is there assigned responsibility for all critical components of the EMS (such as identification of environmental aspects or achieving stated objectives and targets)? How does the person with authority ensure that designated responsibilities are communicated, understood, and met? Are human, technology, and financial resources dedicated to the EMS? How are such resources made available to individual business units when needed?	Organization charts. Job descriptions. Staffing plans/staffing vacancies. Procedures for task assignments and stop work requests. Actual reporting relationships (versus organization chart). Instances of rewards for outstanding environmental performance. Instances of reprimands for failure to carry out environmental responsibilities. Formal reports by designated environmental officer. Agendas and minutes of management meetings.

Figure 6.6. 4.4.1, structure and responsibility gap analysis.

ISO 14001 requirements	Questions	Data sources
Identification of training needs.	How are training needs identified?	Documented procedure.
All employees whose work may have a significant environmental impact must	Is formal skills training conducted as part of job qualification? Is skills training updated regularly?	Demonstrated practice. Employee training and/or professional development plans.
• Receive appropriate training	How does management ensure that skills training is effective?	Training records. Employee credentials file (resume, education attained, professional
• Be competent	How does management ensure that employees throughout the company understand	licenses and exams, honors and awards).
Procedures to make employees aware of		New employee orientation.
• The importance of conformance with environmental policy and procedures	• The importance of conforming to the environmental policy and procedures?	Attendance at conferences, seminars, workshops.
• Requirements of the EMS	• The requirements of ISO 14001?	Performance reviews.
• Their roles and responsibilities in conforming to the policy, procedures, and EMS requirements	• The potential consequences of departure from established operating procedures?	Response to unusual/ emergency situations.
• Actual or potential significant environmental aspects of their work activities	• Their roles and responsibilities?	
• Environmental benefits of improved personal performance	How does the company ensure that on-site contractors are appropriately and adequately trained?	
• Potential consequences of departure from specified operating procedures		

Figure 6.7. 4.4.2, training, awareness, and competence gap analysis.

ISO 14001 requirements	Questions	Data sources
Procedures for internal communication regarding environmental aspects and the EMS. Procedure for receiving, documenting, and responding to relevant communication from external interested parties regarding environmental aspects and the EMS. Consideration of processes for external communication on significant environmental aspects and a record of the organization's decision.	How is environmental information communicated internally? To whom? What mechanisms/procedures enable employees to share environmental concerns with management? How have employees been made aware of these mechanisms/procedures? How does the company obtain information from external interested parties? How is such information handled (routed, documented, responded to)? What kind of environmental information is provided to external interested parties? To whom? How often?	Internal communication procedures. Internal communication practices, for example, • Newsletters • Bulletin boards/posters • Meetings • Audiotapes/videotapes Employee hot line. Sample communications between management and operating employees, for example, • Policy changes • Routine environmental information • Incident/nonroutine information Interviews with individuals responsible for external communications/public relations.

Figure 6.8. 4.4.3, communication gap analysis.

ISO 14001 requirements	Questions	Data sources
Description of the EMS core elements. Description of the interaction of EMS core elements. Direction to related documentation.	Does the company have a formal description of its EMS? In what form is this description? How has this information been distributed? To whom? How are environmental requirements and responsibilities identified and documented for specific groups, functions, and programs? Does actual practice (as observed during gap analysis) reflect the formal description? If not, what are the discrepancies?	EMS manual. Electronic databases. Documented procedures. Documented work instructions. Records.

Figure 6.9. 4.4.4, EMS documentation gap analysis.

ISO 14001 requirements	Questions	Data sources
Procedures to control all documents required by ISO 14001 to ensure that • They can be located • They are periodically reviewed, revised as necessary, and approved for adequacy • Current versions are in use • Obsolete versions are removed from use • Obsolete versions are suitably identified Documentation shall be • Legible • Dated • Maintained in an orderly manner • Retained for a specified period Procedures concerning creation and modification of various types of documents.	What environmental documents are controlled by procedures? How does the company determine what documents should be retained? How does the company determine what documents should be disposed? How is timely removal/disposal of obsolete documents ensured? How does the company determine whether existing document control procedures are adequate?	Written procedures/practices. Master list/file of documents. Document storage/retrieval systems. Observation of documents for dates, signatures. Comparison of in-use documents with master file for currency/obsolescence.

Figure 6.10. 4.4.5, document control gap analysis.

ISO 14001 requirements	Questions	Data sources
Identification of operations and activities associated with identified significant environmental aspects. Documented procedures to cover situations where their absence could lead to deviations from the environmental policy, objectives, and targets. Stipulated operating criteria in the procedures. Procedures related to the identifiable significant environmental aspects of goods and services used by the organization. Communication of relevant procedures and requirements to suppliers and contractors. Procedures related to the identifiable significant environmental aspects of goods and services used by the organization. Communication of relevant procedures and requirements to suppliers and contractors.	What operations/activities are associated with identified significant environmental aspects (see section 4.2.1)? Does the company have established procedures that address all such operations/activities? Have these been documented? To whom have these instructions/procedures been distributed? How have they been used? How are employee departures from established operating procedures identified? How are they addressed? How does the company evaluate significant environmental aspects related to goods and services that it obtains from suppliers and contractors? Have procedures for acquiring/using such goods and services been established? Are they documented? Have such procedures been communicated to suppliers and contractors? How?	List of operations/activities with environmental aspects. Documented work instructions for relevant operations/activities. List of goods/services with identifiable environmental aspects provided by suppliers and contractors. Performance requirements for suppliers and contractors. Procedures to communicate performance requirements. Procedures/practices to ensure adherence to performance requirements.

Figure 6.11. 4.4.6, operational control gap analysis.

ISO 14001 requirements	Questions	Data sources
Procedures to identify potential for accidents and emergency situations. Procedures to respond to accidents and emergency situations. Procedures for preventing/mitigating the environmental impacts associates with accidents and emergency situations. Review (and revision, if necessary) of procedures after the occurrence of accidents or emergency situations. Periodic testing of procedures where practicable.	What operations/activities could result in accidents or emergency situations? How are employees informed about potential accidents and emergencies and their assigned responsibilities in such situations? Do emergency response employees receive training? What kind? How often? How does the company communicate with off-site emergency response agencies? How are environmental impacts associated with emergency incidents evaluated? Are records kept of emergency incidents? Are possible failure modes and resultant risks identified for new procedures? Are emergency plans tested and updated on a regular basis?	Procedure to identify potential accidents and emergency situations. Written accident/emergency response plan(s). Job descriptions. Training records. Performance evaluations of key individuals. Posting of emergency procedures and evacuation plans. Records of actual incidents. Records of revisions to written plans. Formal communication with external agencies (such as hospitals, police, fire department). Records of drills, tests, exercises.

Figure 6.12. 4.4.7, emergency preparedness and response gap analysis.

ISO 14001 requirements	Questions	Data sources
Documented procedures to monitor and measure key characteristics of the operations and activities that can have a significant environmental impact. Recording of information to track • Performance • Relevant operational controls • Conformance with objectives and targets Records of monitoring equipment calibration. Documented procedure for periodically evaluating compliance with relevant legislation and regulations.	Have specific indicators of environmental performance been identified for every significant environmental impact? Have levels of acceptable/unacceptable environmental performance been identified for each indicator? How does the company record information about • Performance? • Environmental operational controls? • Conformance with objectives and targets? How are unacceptable results acted on? How is monitoring equipment calibrated and maintained? How is such information recorded? How is regulatory compliance monitored, measured, and evaluated?	Environmental performance indicators for • All defined objectives and targets • Operations and activities with significant environmental impacts Data obtained from indicators. Procedures/practices for calibration and maintenance of monitoring equipment. Records of calibration and maintenance. Inspection checklists and logs. Regulatory compliance procedures and protocols. Reports prepared for senior management. Minutes of management meetings.

Figure 6.13. 4.5.1, monitoring and measurement gap analysis.

ISO 14001 requirements	Questions	Data sources
Procedures for defining responsibility and authority to • Handle and investigate nonconformance • Take action to mitigate impacts • Initiate and complete corrective and preventive action Corrective or preventive action shall be appropriate to the magnitude of the problem and commensurate with its impact. Changes in documented procedures resulting from corrective and preventive action shall be recorded.	How is responsibility/ authority for addressing nonconformances defined and communicated? How are nonconformances brought to the attention of the responsible person? How is corrective/preventive action • Determined? • Recorded? • Implemented? • Documented? • Integrated with existing procedures?	Job descriptions. Organization chart. Records of nonconformance. Corrective action requests. Corrective action plans. Written documentation of corrective/preventive actions. Trend analysis and performance indicator reports. Records of revisions to procedures.

Figure 6.14. 4.5.2, nonconformance and corrective and preventive action gap analysis.

ISO 14001 requirements	Questions	Data sources
Procedures for the identification, maintenance, and disposition of environmental records. Environmental records shall be • Legible • Identifiable • Traceable to the relevant activity, product, or service • Readily retrievable • Protected against damage, deterioration, or loss Retention times shall be recorded. Records shall include • Training records • Results of audits • Results of reviews • Demonstrated EMS conformance	What kinds of contractor/supplier/procurement records are retained? Do such records contain information about environmental responsibilities and accountabilities? Do such records contain information about contractor/supplier environmental performance?	List of records and their retention times. Written procedures. Demonstrated practices. Storage and retrieval systems. Observation of records for dates, signatures.

Figure 6.15. 4.5.3, records gap analysis.

ISO 14001 requirements	Questions	Data sources
Program and procedures for periodic EMS audits to • Determine whether the EMS conforms to all requirements • Determine whether the EMS has been properly implemented and maintained • Provide information on the results of EMS audits to management Audit program and schedule shall be based on • Environmental importance of the activity concerned • Results of previous audits Audit procedures shall cover • Audit scope • Frequency • Methodologies • Responsibilities for conducting audits • Responsibilities for reporting results	Is there a formal EMS audit program? How often are EMS audits conducted? Is this sufficient? How are EMS audit findings communicated internally? To whom? How are EMS audit findings communicated externally? To whom? How are EMS audit results acted on? Is there a formal system for top management review of EMS audit findings and responses?	Audit procedures. Audit program. Procedures for reporting EMS nonconformances. EMS audit reports.

Figure 6.16. 4.5.4, EMS audit gap analysis.

ISO 14001 requirements	Questions	Data sources
Periodic documented review (by top management) of the EMS.	How does management obtain information concerning • Emerging environmental issues? • Regulatory developments? • Activities and effectiveness of environmental personnel? • Nature and adequacy of nonhuman resources? • Environmental expenditures and cost savings? • Individual incidents, accidents, and emergency situations? • Concerns and perceptions of key internal and external interested parties? How does performance relative to environmental objectives and targets influence decisions about the EMS? How is new/revised environmental information integrated into company environmental policies, objectives, and targets? Into other planning processes?	Management review reports. Records of management deliberations such as • Agendas • Meeting minutes • Action plans • Revisions to policies, procedures • New or revised objectives and targets

Figure 6.17. 4.6, management review gap analysis.

Chapter 7

Integrating ISO 14001 with an Existing Environmental Management System

ISO 14001 allows organizations the flexibility to implement the EMS as broadly or narrowly as management deems appropriate. It can be applied across an entire corporation, to selected business units or divisions, or even to specific facilities within a business unit. ISO 14001 also can be implemented for a single production process regardless of the number of facilities involved or a business function that cuts across several divisions.

ISO 14001 also applies to organizations of all sizes. Initially, ISO/TC 207 debated the need to develop a separate standard for small and medium-sized enterprises. Ultimately, it concluded that the elements depicted in ISO 14001 should apply to any EMS regardless of company size; the implementation is what differs from company to company. The scale of effort should be commensurate with the nature of the company's business and its environmental aspects and impacts. In actual practice, implementing ISO 14001 within a single facility or operating unit of a large corporation is comparable to implementing the standard within small and medium-sized enterprises.

Once an organization has performed gap analysis for that portion of its operations that will be subject to ISO 14001, it is in a position to identify whether its EMS conforms to the requirements of ISO 14001 and, if not, where major and minor deficiencies exist. This chapter is designed to help companies implement the various elements of ISO 14001 by presenting the experiences of United Technologies Corporation (UTC).

Decisions made and actions taken by UTC are described for each ISO 14001 element. The approach taken by UTC is not necessarily appropriate for other organizations. Any approach must reflect the status of a company's existing EMS and the environmental aspects and impacts with which it must contend. It is anticipated, however, that UTC's experiences—with practices that were successfully employed as well as those that fell into the category of "if we had it to do over"— will be instructive to others undertaking a similar effort. The chapter is organized according to the ISO 14001 elements, thereby enabling readers to focus on those areas of greatest interest.

United Technologies Corporation

United Technologies Corporation is a $22 billion corporation that provides a broad range of high-technology products and support services to customers in the aerospace, building, and automotive industries worldwide. UTC's best-known products include Pratt & Whitney aircraft engines, Otis elevators and escalators, Carrier heating and air conditioning systems, Sikorsky helicopters, Hamilton Standard aerospace systems, and UT Automotive components and systems. UTC also supplies equipment and services to the U.S. space program. It has 170,600 employees and more than 245 major manufacturing facilities in 34 countries.

In 1991, UTC established a formal EMS to address several concerns.

- Lack of effective management methods to ensure compliance with environmental and safety regulations and poor results in some divisions.

- Significant environmental emissions—When UTC began to address this problem in the late 1980s, it was emitting 400 tons/week of hazardous waste and 600 tons/month of reportable chemical releases in the United States alone.

- Employee health and safety—Lost time injury rates in 1990, measured in terms of both incidence and severity, were more than twice those of companies of comparable size and type.

In 1993, UTC recognized that a number of elements in its existing EMS required improvement. Mindful of the work being done by ISO/TC 207 and for several other reasons, UTC deferred revising its EMS until ISO 14001 was far enough along that it could be integrated. The following section describes UTC's progress in making ISO 14001 a corporate reality.

United Technologies Corporation and ISO 14001

UTC employs a decentralized organizational structure with distinct roles and responsibilities in relation to ISO 14001. With respect to ISO 14000 the overall goal of UTC's corporate EHS office is to provide tools, education, training, and guidance that will assist operating units seeking ISO 14000 certification.

Initially, the corporate EHS office performed gap analysis between the ISO 14001 requirements and UTC's existing EMS. It also provided briefings and served as a general resource to relevant management and councils throughout the corporation. Ongoing efforts include assisting the operating units by coordinating efforts among operating units through macrolevel environmental policies, revising the UTC EMS to consider ISO 14001 requirements (among other factors), and overseeing interdepartmental procedures such as training of internal ISO 14001 auditors.

The next level in the UTC hierarchy comprises individual companies or operating units, such as Carrier and Pratt & Whitney. All operating units must implement ISO 14001 to the extent that UTC's revised EMS so requires. However, each operating unit will determine whether it wishes to pursue ISO 14000 certification. It is anticipated that operating unit decisions will reflect customer expectations and market conditions.

The third tier in the UTC organization encompasses individual facilities within an operating unit (also referred to as operating unit locations).

At present, there are no plans to make ISO 14000 registration a corporationwide requirement. UTC's existing EHS management system will continue to be the driving standard for achieving environmental excellence at UTC because it

- Is a mandatory requirement.
- Has been successfully disseminated throughout UTC's facilities worldwide.
- Goes beyond environment to include health and safety.
- Meets or goes beyond the intent of ISO 14001. The existing EMS is being revised to identify and incorporate ISO 14001 elements that were not initially addressed.

UTC believes that any facility conforming to the corporation's revised EMS will fulfill the requirements of ISO 14000.

4.2, Environmental Policy

UTC has had an environmental policy, Human and Natural Resource Protection Policy and Policy Principles, since 1989 (see Figure 7.1). Additionally, UTC requires that each operating unit location have a written policy statement that clearly communicates management's commitment to environmental improvement to the workforce.

In 1995, UTC decided to revise its environmental policy to

- Reflect progress achieved in environmental, health, and safety management

- Reflect additional corporate commitments, such as product stewardship and external communication

- Include additional elements contained in industry codes of practice that UTC has signed

- Ensure that it is a dynamic and guiding document

It is the policy of United Technologies Corporation to provide its employees with a workplace safe from recognized occupational hazards and to protect the natural environment. The corporation will conduct its worldwide operations in a manner that safeguards employee health and safety and the environment, and in so doing, abide by all applicable laws, regulations and internal standards.

The corporation will participate with governmental agencies, trade associations and others to develop equitable laws, regulations and standards, and work constructively with government authorities in their legitimate efforts for the protection of human and natural resources.

Safe working conditions and environmental protection are integral components of our business strategy. Therefore, management at all levels is responsible for identifying and attaining goals within each organization to ensure implementation of this policy.

The corporation will provide management with professional assistance to help meet its human and natural resource protection goals.

Each employee plays an important role by following established procedures and recommending improved practices where appropriate.

Source: Reprinted with permission from United Technologies Corporation.

Figure 7.1. UTC's original environmental policy, 1989.

Preliminary work began in July 1995, and was completed during the third quarter of 1996 (see Figure 7.2). It was approved by UTC's CEO and board of directors.

Internal communication of the revised environmental policy is accomplished through two avenues. Upon publication, it was distributed to all employees. New employees are exposed to the language

---

United Technologies Corporation will not be satisfied until its workplace is safe from hazards, its employees are injury free, its products and services are safe, and its commitment and record in protecting the natural environment are unmatched.

Commitments

Eliminate all employee injuries by making the workplace free from hazards and unsafe actions.

Drive pollutants in manufacturing processes to the lowest achievable levels.

Conserve natural resources in the design, manufacture, use and disposal of products and delivery of services.

Establish safety and environmental protection standards that both comply with local laws and go beyond, when necessary, to achieve the goals of this policy.

Hold operating managers accountable for safety and environmental performance and for providing leadership and required resources.

Require all employees to comply with these standards.

Support

Quantify safety and environmental goals; measure progress regularly; report progress to the UTC Board of Directors, employees and communities; and respond to suggestions and needs of others.

Develop technologies and methods to assure safe workplaces worldwide and to protect the environment, and promulgate these outside UTC.

Make safety and environmental considerations priorities in new product development and investment decisions, and in our dealings with contractors and suppliers.

Work with government and industry associations to advance laws and regulations supporting these goals.

Source: Reprinted with permission from United Technologies Corporation.

Figure 7.2. UTC's revised environmental policy, 1996.

and intent of the policy through UTC's new employee orientation program.

The policy is also widely available to external interested parties. Since 1992, UTC has published an annual EHS progress report that is both printed and available on the Internet. The environmental policy is contained in every report. The 1995 progress report and those that follow contain the revised policy. Additionally, the policy is available upon request.

4.3.1, Environmental Aspects

UTC has several procedures in place, some since 1992, that fulfill the requirements of this element.

• UTC standard practice (SP) 005, "Multimedia EHS Self-Assessments," was established in 1992 to provide guidance for conducting an annual EHS self-assessment. It applies to all UTC operating unit locations worldwide.

• SP 006, "Air Pollution Prevention and Control," also established in 1992, addresses the basic elements of an air pollution prevention and control program. It provides guidance for each UTC facility to inventory its air emissions, ensure regulatory compliance, and develop a management system that assimilates evolving air laws and regulatory requirements without reducing operational flexibility.

• SP 009, "Water Pollution Prevention and Control," was established in 1995 to minimize the impact of UTC operations on surface water and ground water. This standard applies to all UTC locations worldwide where no local water requirements exist or where existing requirements are less stringent than those in the United States. In locations with more stringent local requirements, the more stringent requirements apply.

Waste and emissions inventories were conducted at UTC U.S. facilities beginning in 1988. Currently, UTC is conducting waste and emission inventories at its non-U.S. operations and setting voluntary reduction goals for those wastes and releases.

Once environmental aspects are identified, their impacts are determined through process mapping, EHS hazard identification, and risk ranking. These procedures were established by UTC corporate EHS staff, operating unit EHS professionals, and outside consultants.

Environmental impact procedures are used selectively for determining the environmental impacts of existing, modified, and proposed manufacturing processes. Risk ranking helps identify the appropriate scope for assessing impacts. Individual facilities usually assess their respective impacts on a local and regional basis; operating unit executive management assesses impacts on a global basis.

4.3.2, Legal and Other Requirements

Legal Requirements. All UTC operating units are responsible for conducting all of their operations in a manner that complies with all applicable laws and regulations. UTC has both formal and informal procedures for identifying and providing access to legal requirements that apply to the environmental aspects of its activities, products, and services.

UTC's current, primary, formal procedure for identifying and providing access to applicable legal requirements is the UTC legal and regulatory requirements (LRR) database. Currently, there are two versions of the LRR database. One of these, UTC's LRR federal database, is maintained by the UTC corporate EHS department, which is responsible for screening the *Federal Register* and identifying for UTC operating units all of the new U.S. federal laws and regulations (plus all new state laws and regulations that involve federal laws or regulations) that apply to the environmental aspects of UTC's activities, products, and services.

The other, UTC's Connecticut state database, is maintained by the UTC corporate government affairs department, which is responsible for screening all new laws and regulations issued by the state of Connecticut and identifying for UTC operating units with operations in Connecticut those new laws and regulations that apply to the environmental (or any other) aspects of UTC's activities, products, and services.

Both versions of the LRR database are periodically updated on an ongoing basis, and new applicable items are distributed electronically to affected UTC operating unit EHS departments.

There also are a variety of informal procedures for identifying and providing access to applicable environmental laws and regulations. In general, each operating unit's EHS department, with support as needed or appropriate from the legal department and other functions, is responsible for identifying such laws and regulations and providing access.

Other Requirements. There are two basic types of other requirements that apply to the environmental aspects of UTC's activities, products, and services to which UTC does, or might in the future, subscribe: external standards issued by nongovernmental organizations, and internal standards issued by UTC management. External standards fall into two categories: those to which UTC subscribes on a corporatewide basis applicable to all operating units; and those to which only specific operating units subscribe.

Two external standards to which UTC subscribes on a corporatewide basis are the International Chamber of Commerce (ICC) Business Charter for Sustainable Development and the Public Environmental Reporting Initiative. The procedure by which UTC subscribes to such requirements is a formal process involving review and approval of the standard by the UTC EHS council, which is comprised of the senior EHS officer of each operating unit and senior corporate EHS management. Each EHS council member is responsible for identifying and providing access to the requirements of these standards to affected personnel within his or her operating unit.

An external standard that is subscribed to on an operating unit basis is the U.S. EPA Green Lights Program, which has been implemented by UTC's Carrier air conditioning unit.

With respect to internal corporatewide standards, the current, primary, formal procedure for identifying and providing access to the requirements of applicable standards is the issuance of a UTC SP by the UTC Corporate EHS department, based on review and approval of such SP by the UTC EHS council. The broadest internal corporatewide standard subscribed to by UTC is SP 001, which sets forth the elements of UTC's model EHS management system. As with the other standards mentioned, each EHS council member is responsible for identifying and providing access to the requirements of these standards to affected personnel within his or her operating unit. UTC plans to issue an updated and revised version of SP 001 by the end of 1996.

4.3.3, Objectives and Targets

Objectives and targets are established by the vice president of EHS and the EHS council, who make recommendations to UTC and operating unit executive management. Recommendations reflect the corporate environmental policy and significant environmental aspects and impacts.

Employee input is solicited by consulting with EHS oversight committees at each operating unit facility, line management, and union representatives. When recommended objectives and targets are approved for the corporation, they cascade down to operating units and individual facilities.

Measurable indicators are established for many targets. For example, waste reduction target indicators include pounds of hazardous waste generated, chemical releases, and air releases (see Figure 7.3). Once established, objectives and targets are reviewed annually and revised where appropriate.

4.3.4, Environmental Management Program

Senior management at each operating unit facility is responsible for achieving designated objectives and targets. There is wide variability in how this is communicated between operating unit corporate staff, facility professionals, and facility line management.

Indicator	Target reduction, 2000	Interim target, 1997
Hazardous waste (United States)	80% from 1988 base year	65%
Hazardous waste (non–United States)	50% from 1995 base year	25%
Chemical releases (United States)	95% from 1988 base year	90%
Air releases (non–United States)	50% from 1995 base year	25%

Source: Reprinted with permission from United Technologies Corporation.

Figure 7.3. Selected waste reduction target indicators.

Allocation of resources for achieving objectives and targets also varies among facilities. Some develop specific EHS budgets for designated objectives and targets; others operate from the general budget. Allocation of technical resources also differs. In some instances, EHS professionals are dedicated to meeting objectives and targets; in others, responsibility is shared by functions such as quality, maintenance, and human resources.

The UTC Assurance Program assesses effectiveness in achieving objectives and targets. It has a number of protocols that are used to evaluate performance. Where performance is deemed inadequate, environmental management programs are modified by the appropriate operating units and reassessed by the Assurance Program.

UTC has identified the need to strengthen incentives for achieving targets as an area for improvement. It hopes to reduce findings of inadequate performance and, therefore, the allocation of resources to corrective action. In the spirit of continual improvement, UTC is striving to get it right the first time.

4.4.1, Structure and Responsibility

UTC is a diversified, decentralized corporation made up of six major operating units plus a research center. The EHS effort at each of these units is led by its president and a senior EHS officer reporting directly to the president.

The vice president of EHS was appointed by UTC's CEO as the corporation's top environmental officer. In that capacity, she provides strategic direction to UTC on EHS issues. At least twice per year, she reports to the board of directors and presidents' council (comprised of presidents of all operating units).

Additional responsibilities are designated at various levels within UTC.

- The board of directors has designated EHS issues for periodic review by its public issues review committee.

- Each operating unit appoints its own member to the EHS council, a group of senior EHS officers of the operating units.

- Each facility has an EHS coordinator and an EHS oversight committee. Further, each facility must ensure that the roles and responsibilities of line and staff are clearly communicated and understood.

4.4.2, Training, Awareness, and Competence

Training needs are identified by operating units. Specific identification of training needs comes from regulatory and legal requirements. Additionally, the UTC EMS requires that training initiatives must address the inherent risks present at each facility. The UTC corporate office provides the lead in identifying new global issues of concern and may conduct training initially.

Training for employees with specific needs varies by operating unit and reflects the specific area of training that is required. However, initial training must include both an orientation to the facility's EHS program and job-specific training. Additional training is initiated when employees transfer to new jobs or an operating process changes.

General awareness training is accomplished through new employee orientation and the provision of internal courses including the following:

- Environment, Health, and Safety 101
- Environmental management for operations managers
- Environmental management for line management
- Toolbox talks (for shop floor employees)

Each facility establishes an annual plan that delineates who will be trained, the training topics, and the dates that training will be conducted.

Training tracking is the responsibility of operating units and emphasizes employee participation in training courses. UTC requires that training records include, at a minimum, attendance sheets, a detailed course outline, and the dates of training.

Although the UTC EMS also mandates verification that learning has occurred as a result of training, training effectiveness is not determined in any comprehensive manner. Where verification is sought, on-the-job observation tends to be the method of choice.

4.4.3, Communication

UTC has an extensive communication system. Employees and external interested parties may receive information about EHS issues in the following publications.

- *UTC Environment, Health, and Safety Progress Report* (published annually since 1992)
- *UTC Corporate Annual Report*
- *UTC Site Remediation News*
- *UTC Waste Lessons*

Most of this information is also available online through UTC and operating unit home pages on the World Wide Web.

Additional information is communicated to employees through a variety of sources such as operating unit newsletters, bulletin boards in common and work areas, and regulatory updates.

4.4.4, Environmental Management System Documentation

UTC has developed extensive guidelines for developing and maintaining EMS and related documentation. However, individual facilities have flexibility in how they maintain such documentation.

Regardless of the manner in which EMS documentation is maintained (for example, a written manual, or electronic database), it is supposed to be both integrated with other facility procedures and identifiable. Employees are able to access EMS documentation in a variety of ways, including bulletin boards, central files, internal memoranda and newsletters, and by consulting with EHS professionals, human resources and legal departments, and facility management.

4.4.5, Document Control

Controlled environmental documents include material safety data sheets, report forms, permits, notices of violations and citations, and audit reports. Procedures vary among operating units, and may be heavily dependent on whether the facility is ISO 9000 certified.

Most controlled documents are available to employees through the appropriate EHS professional or facility manager. Sensitive documents are retained by the legal or human resources departments.

4.4.6, Operational Control

Manufacturing operations generally have been analyzed for environmental aspects and their impacts. Service activities have not been analyzed in a consistent fashion throughout UTC. Product stewardship analysis is in its infancy at UTC. As described previously, process mapping, EHS hazard identification, and risk ranking are used to document the environmental impact of specific operations.

At present, UTC does not have a corporate initiative to identify the significant environmental aspects of the goods and services provided by external contractors and suppliers. Such aspects currently are assessed by operating units and facilities in an ad hoc fashion, typically in response to external party concerns or the need to manufacture product in a more efficient manner.

Efforts to date have focused on treatment-storage-disposal facilities (TSDFs) for various types of hazardous wastes. UTC has reduced the number of TSDFs used; suppliers of disposable services wanting to stay on UTC's preferred list must comply with UTC audit standards.

Other types of contractors are notified about internal EHS policies and procedures prior to arriving at UTC facilities. The scope of issues addressed varies by operating unit and facilities.

4.4.7, Emergency Preparedness and Response

Every UTC facility is required to have formal written procedures such as an emergency plan. Facility EHS professionals work with facility management and local authorities to establish procedures for the following:

- Identifying potential accidents and emergency situations

- Responding to potential accidents and emergency situations

- Preventing and mitigating the environmental impacts associated with potential accidents and emergency situations

Each facility is supposed to conduct an annual test of emergency procedures, but adherence to this requirement varies by operating unit and facility.

4.5.1, *Monitoring and Measurement*

The environmental performance associated with corporatewide objectives and targets is tracked by UTC's corporate EHS office. Operating unit–level and facility-level goals in support of corporate initiatives are tracked by the appropriate EHS professionals.

UTC employs the environmental performance indicators generally used by U.S. industry, such as toxic release inventory data, Superfund sites, and number of notices of violation. However, UTC has also established other environmental performance indicators such as number of approved TSDFs, number of assurance reviews, and number of closed-out action plans. Compliance audits are used to evaluate compliance with environmental regulations.

4.5.2, *Nonconformance and Corrective and Preventive Action*

Facility and operating unit procedures have been established for handling noncompliance with environmental regulations and UTC standards. Action plans generated by compliance audits and assurance audits are monitored to ensure that all open corrective and preventive actions are implemented and closed.

4.5.3, *Records*

UTC requires that facilities maintain the following records.

- EHS training records
- Accident/injury/illness statistics
- Incident investigations
- EHS self-inspection/audit reports
- EHS awareness meetings
- Internal EHS studies
- Air emissions and water discharges
- Solid and hazardous wastes
- Chemical inventory and usage

Procedures to prepare, maintain, and dispose of such records vary by operating unit.

Environmental records are typically maintained in a central location. Employee access is obtained through the legal department, facility management, or EHS professionals. Permits are generally maintained on equipment.

4.5.4, Environmental Management System Audit

At the direction of UTC's CEO, the corporate EHS office developed procedures, protocols, action plans, tracking systems, and rating systems—collectively referred to as the assurance review program—to audit the EMS. Audit results are shared with employees at different organizational levels.

- Corporate
  - —Vice president, EHS
  - —Director, assurance review program
- Operating unit
  - —President
  - —Assurance coordinator
  - —EHS council representative
- Facility
  - —Manager
  - —Relevant staff

4.6, Management Review

UTC requires an annual EMS review at the facility level. At a minimum, those involved in the review are the facility manager, facility EHS coordinator, and representatives from human resources, the unions, operations, and training. The review is documented in minutes from management review meetings.

Conclusion

UTC endorsed integration of ISO 14001 into its EMS because it provides an internationally recognized vehicle that enables UTC to demonstrate its ongoing commitment to environmental leadership. The language of ISO 14001 enables UTC to easily explain to others what it is already doing, aids in technology transfer, and helps convey the importance of UTC's EMS to line management.

UTC's own EMS, which is mandatory at all facilities, is more substantive than ISO 14001. For example, ISO 14001 requires organizations to *commit to* regulatory compliance; UTC's EMS *requires* compliance. Therefore, UTC will not mandate implementation of ISO 14001, which is less stringent. Operating units are encouraged to implement ISO 14001 if they perceive that implementation will provide value (for example, by fulfilling customer expectations).

UTC's approach may be instructive for those organizations with an existing EMS. Integration of ISO 14001 with an existing EMS rather than wholesale replacement can enhance environmental management and ensure continuity at a reasonable cost.

Section III

Comparing ISO 14001 to Other Standards

This section compares ISO 14001 to the requirements embodied in a number of other standards.

The first component of this section compares areas of overlap between ISO 14001 and ISO 9001. Companies that wish to integrate ISO 14001 with an existing ISO 9000 initiative can readily identify ISO 9000 elements that are appropriate for their ISO 14001 environmental management system.

Second, this section compares ISO 14001 to three EMS standards of particular interest to U.S. companies and others. First is the European EMAS. Second is Great Britain's BS 7750, developed in 1992 in anticipation of EMAS and revised in 1994. Third is NSF 110, developed by U.S.-based NSF International. If ANSI successfully adopts ISO 14001 as the U.S. national EMS standard, NSF will review the need for continued publication of NSF 110.

Third, this section delineates the similarities between ISO 14001 and the International Chamber of Commerce (ICC) Business Charter for Sustainable Development. The ICC Business Charter represents a code of practice rather than a standard; however, its endorsement by more than 1000 signatories suggests that many of the companies that implement ISO 14001 will want to integrate the implementation effort with their ICC Business Charter activities.

Finally, ISO 14001 is compared to three industry codes of practice—the American Petroleum Institute Strategies for Today's Environmental Partnership (API-STEP); the American Textile Manufacturers Institute (ATMI) Encouraging Environmental Excellence (E3) Program; and the Chemical Manufacturers Association (CMA) Responsible Care® program. Readers from other industries may find the similarities between ISO 14001 and industry-specific recommendations regarding environmental performance instructive.

Comparison of Selected Elements
of ISO 9001 and ISO 14001

ISO 9001

4.1.1 Quality policy

The supplier's management with executive responsibility shall define and document its policy for quality, including objectives for quality and its commitment to quality. The quality policy shall be relevant to the supplier's organizational goals and the expectations and needs of its customers. The supplier shall ensure that this policy is understood, implemented, and maintained at all levels of the organization.

ISO 14001

4.2 Environmental policy

Top management shall define the organization's environmental policy and ensure that it

a) is appropriate to the nature, scale and environmental impacts of its activities, products or services;

b) includes a commitment to continual improvement and prevention of pollution;

c) includes a commitment to comply with relevant environmental legislation and regulations, and with other requirements to which the organization subscribes;

d) provides the framework for setting and reviewing environmental objectives and targets;

e) is documented, implemented and maintained and communicated to all employees;

f) is available to the public.

Reprinted with permission from ASQC, Milwaukee, Wisconsin.

Reprinted with permission from ASQC, Milwaukee, Wisconsin.

4.1.2.1 Responsibility and authority

The responsibility, authority, and the interrelation of personnel who manage, perform, and verify work affecting quality shall be defined and documented, particularly for personnel who need the organizational freedom and authority to:

a) initiate action to prevent the occurrence of any nonconformities relating to product, process, and quality system;

b) identify and record any problems relating to the product, process, and quality system;

c) initiate, recommend, or provide solutions through designated channels;

d) verify the implementation of solutions;

e) control further processing, delivery, or installation of nonconforming product until the deficiency or unsatisfactory condition has been corrected.

4.1.3 Management review

The supplier's management with executive responsibility shall review the quality system at defined intervals sufficient to ensure its continuing suitability and effectiveness in satisfying the requirements of this American National Standard and the supplier's stated quality policy and objectives. Records of such reviews shall be maintained.

4.4.1 Structure and responsibility

Roles, responsibility and authorities shall be defined, documented and communicated in order to facilitate effective environmental management.

Management shall provide resources essential to the implementation and control of the environmental management system. Resources include human resources and specialized skills, technology and financial resources.

The organization's top management shall appoint (a) specific management representative(s) who, irrespective of other responsibilities, shall have defined roles, responsibilities and authority for

a) ensuring that environmental management system requirements are established, implemented and maintained in accordance with this International Standard;

b) reporting on the performance of the environmental management system to top management for review and as a basis for improvement of the environmental management system.

4.6 Management review

The organization's top management shall, at intervals it determines, review the environmental management system to ensure its continuing suitability, adequacy and effectiveness. The management review process shall ensure that the necessary information is collected to allow management to carry out this evaluation. This review shall be documented.

The management review shall address the possible need for changes to policy, objectives and other elements of the environmental management system, in the light of environmental management system audit results, changing circumstances and the commitment to continual improvement

4.2.1 General

The supplier shall establish, document, and maintain a quality system as a means of ensuring that product conforms to specified requirements. The supplier shall prepare a quality manual covering the requirements of this American National Standard. The quality manual shall include or make reference to the quality-system procedures and outline the structure of the documentation used in the quality system.

4.2.3 Quality planning

The supplier shall define and document how the requirements for quality will be met. Quality planning shall be consistent with all other requirements of a supplier's quality system and shall be documented in a format to suit the supplier's method of operation. The supplier shall give consideration to the following activities, as appropriate, in meeting the specified requirements for products, projects, or contracts:

a) the preparation of quality plans;

.
.
.

h) the identification and preparation of quality records.

4.4.4 Environmental management system documentation

The organization shall establish and maintain information, in paper or electronic form, to

a) describe the core elements of the management system and their interaction;

b) provide direction to related documentation.

4.3.4 Environmental management program(s)

The organization shall establish and maintain (a) programme(s) for achieving its objectives and targets. It shall include

a) designation of responsibility for achieving objectives and targets at each relevant function and level of the organization;

b) the means and time-frame by which they are to be achieved.

If a project relates to new developments and new or modified activities, products or services, programme(s) shall be amended where relevant to ensure that environmental management applies to such projects.

4.5 Document and Data Control

4.5.1 General

The supplier shall establish and maintain documented procedures to control all documents and data that relate to the requirements of this American National Standard including, to the extent applicable, documents of external origin such as standards and customer drawings.

4.5.2 Document and data approval and issue

The documents and data shall be reviewed and approved for adequacy by authorized personnel prior to issue. A master list or equivalent document-control procedure identifying the current revision status of documents shall be established and be readily available to preclude the use of invalid and/or obsolete documents.

This control shall ensure that:

a) the pertinent issues of appropriate documents are available at all locations where operations essential to the effective functioning of the quality system are performed;

b) invalid and/or obsolete documents are promptly removed from all points of issue or use, or otherwise assured against unintended use;

c) any obsolete documents retained for legal and/or knowledge-preservation purposes are suitably identified.

4.4.5 Document control

The organization shall establish and maintain procedures for controlling all documents required by this International Standard to ensure that

a) they can be located;

b) they are periodically reviewed, revised as necessary and approved for adequacy by authorized personnel;

c) the current versions of relevant documents are available at all locations where operations essential to the effective functioning of the environmental management system are performed;

d) obsolete documents are promptly removed from all points of issue and points of use, or otherwise assured against unintended use;

e) any obsolete documents retained for legal and/or knowledge preservation purposes are suitably identified.

Documentation shall be legible, dated (with dates of revision), and readily identifiable, maintained in an orderly manner and retained for a specified period. Procedures and responsibilities shall be established and maintained concerning the creation and modification of the various types of document.

4.5.3 Document and data changes

Changes to documents and data shall be reviewed and approved by the same functions/organizations that performed the original review and approval, unless specifically designated otherwise. The designated functions/organizations shall have access to pertinent background information upon which to base their review and approval.

Where practicable, the nature of the change shall be identified in the document or the appropriate attachments.

4.9 Process control

The supplier shall identify and plan the production, installation and servicing processes which directly affect quality and shall ensure that these processes are carried out under controlled conditions. Controlled conditions shall include the following:

a) documented procedures defining the manner of production, installation, and servicing, where the absence of such procedures could adversely affect quality; . . .

4.4.6 Operational control

The organization shall identify those operations and activities that are associated with the identified significant environmental aspects in line with its policy, objectives and targets. The organization shall plan these activities, including maintenance, in order to ensure that they are carried out under specified conditions by

a) establishing and maintaining documented procedures to cover situations where their absence could lead to deviations from the environmental policy and the objectives and targets;

b) stipulating operating criteria in the procedures;

c) establishing and maintaining procedures related to the identifiable significant environmental aspects of goods and services used by the organization and communicating relevant procedures and requirements to suppliers and contractors.

4.11.2 Control procedure
The supplier shall: . . .

b) identify all inspection, measuring, and test equipment that can affect product quality, and calibrate and adjust them at prescribed intervals, or prior to use, against certified equipment having a known valid relationship to internationally or nationally recognized standards. Where no such standards exist, the basis used for calibration shall be documented;

e) maintain calibration records for inspection, measuring, and test equipment; . . .

4.14 Corrective and Preventive Action

4.14.1 General
The supplier shall establish and maintain documented procedures for implementing corrective and preventive action.

Any corrective or preventive action taken to eliminate the causes or actual or potential nonconformities shall be to a degree appropriate to the magnitude of problems and commensurate with the risks encountered.

The supplier shall implement and record any changes to the documented procedures resulting from corrective and preventive action.

4.5.1 Monitoring and measurement
The organization shall establish and maintain documented procedures to monitor and measure, on a regular basis, the key characteristics of its operations and activities that can have a significant impact on the environment. This shall include the recording of information to track performance, relevant operational controls and conformance with the organization's objectives and targets.

Monitoring equipment shall be calibrated and maintained and records of this process shall be retained according to the organization's procedures.

The organization shall establish and maintain a documented procedure for periodically evaluating compliance with relevant environmental legislation and regulations.

4.5.2 Nonconformance and corrective and preventive action
The organization shall establish and maintain procedures for defining responsibility and authority for handling and investigating nonconformance, taking action to mitigate any impacts caused and for initiating and completing corrective and preventive action.

Any corrective or preventive action taken to eliminate the causes of actual and potential nonconformances shall be appropriate to the magnitude of problems and commensurate with the environmental impact encountered.

The organization shall implement and record any changes in the documented procedures resulting from corrective and preventive action.

4.16 Control of quality records
The suppliers shall establish and maintain documented procedures for identification, collection, indexing, access, filing, storage, maintenance, and disposition of quality records.

Quality records shall be maintained to demonstrate conformance to specified requirements and the effective operation of the quality system. Pertinent quality records from the subcontractor shall be an element of these data.

All quality records shall be legible and shall be stored and retained in such a way that they are readily retrievable in facilities that provide a suitable environment to prevent damage or deterioration and to prevent loss. Retention times of quality records shall be established and recorded. Where agreed contractually, quality records shall be made available for evaluation by the customer or the customer's representative for an agreed period.

4.5.3 Records
The organization shall establish and maintain procedures for the identification, maintenance and disposition of environmental records. These records shall include training records and the results of audits and reviews.

Environmental records shall be legible, identifiable and traceable to the activity, product or service involved. Environmental records shall be stored and maintained in such a way that they are readily retrievable and protected against damage, deterioration or loss. Their retention times shall be established and recorded.

Records shall be maintained, as appropriate to the system and to the organization, to demonstrate conformance to the requirements of this International Standard.

4.17 Internal quality audits

The supplier shall establish and maintain documented procedures for planning and implementing internal quality audits to verify whether quality activities and related results comply with planned arrangements and to determine the effectiveness of the quality system.

Internal quality audits shall be scheduled on the basis of the status and importance of the activity to be audited and shall be carried out by personnel independent of those having direct responsibility for the activity being audited.

The results of the audits shall be recorded and brought to the attention of the personnel having responsibility in the area audited. The management personnel responsible for the area shall take timely corrective action on deficiencies found during the audit.

Follow-up audit activities shall verify and record the implementation and effectiveness of the corrective action taken.

4.5.4 Environmental management system audit

The organization shall establish and maintain (a) programme(s) and procedures for periodic environmental management system audits to be carried out, in order to

a) determine whether or not the environmental management system

   1) conforms to planned arrangements for environmental management including the requirements of this International Standard; and

   2) has been properly implemented and maintained; and

b) provide information on the results of audits to management.

The organization's audit programme, including any schedule, shall be based on the environmental importance of the activity concerned and the results of previous audits. In order to be comprehensive, the audit procedures shall cover the audit scope, frequency and methodologies, as well as the responsibilities and requirements for conducting audits and reporting results.

4.18 Training

The supplier shall establish and maintain documented procedures for identifying training needs and provide for the training of all personnel performing activities affecting quality. Personnel performing specific assigned tasks shall be qualified on the basis of appropriate education, training and/or experience, as required. Appropriate records of training shall be maintained.

4.4.2 Training, awareness and competence

The organization shall identify training needs. It shall require that all personnel whose work may create a significant impact upon the environment, have received appropriate training.

It shall establish and maintain procedures to make its employees or members at each relevant function and level aware of

a) the importance of conformance with the environmental policy and procedures and with the requirements of the environmental management system;

b) the significant environmental impacts, actual or potential, of their work activities and the environmental benefits of improved personal performance;

c) their roles and responsibilities in achieving conformance with the environmental policy and procedures and with the requirements of the environmental management system, including emergency preparedness and response requirements;

d) the potential consequences of departure from specified operating procedures.

Personnel performing the tasks which can cause significant environmental impacts shall be competent on the basis of appropriate education, training and/or experience.

Comparison of EMAS Annex I
and ISO 14001

EMAS Annex I

A. Environmental policies, objectives and programmes

1. The company environmental policy, and the programme for the site, shall be established in writing. Associated documents will explain how the environmental programme and the management system at the site relate to the policy and systems of the company as a whole.

2. The company environmental policy shall be adopted and periodically reviewed, in particular in the light of environmental audits, and revised as appropriate, at the highest management level. It shall be communicated to the company's personnel and be publicly available.

3. The company's environmental policy shall be based on the principles of action in Section D.

The policy will aim, in addition to providing for compliance with all relevant regulatory requirements regarding the environment, at the continual improvement of environmental performance.

The environmental policy and the programme for the site shall address, in particular, the issue in section C.

ISO 14001

4.2 Environmental policy

Top management shall define the organization's environmental policy and ensure that it

a) is appropriate to the nature, scale and environmental impacts of its activities, products or services;

b) includes a commitment to continual improvement and prevention of pollution;

c) includes a commitment to comply with relevant environmental legislation and regulations, and with other requirements to which the organization subscribes;

d) provides the framework for setting and reviewing environmental objectives and targets;

e) is documented, implemented and maintained and communicated to all employees;

f) is available to the public.

Source: Council Regulation (EEC) No 1836/93, Official Journal of the European Communities, No. L 168/1-18, July 10, 1993.

Reprinted with permission from ASQC, Milwaukee, Wisconsin.

4. Environmental objectives

The company shall specify its environmental objectives at all relevant levels within the company. The objectives shall be consistent with the environmental policy and shall quantify wherever practicable the commitment to continual improvement in environmental performance over defined time scales.

4.3.3 Objectives and targets

The organization shall establish and maintain documented environmental objectives and targets, at each relevant function and level within the organization.

When establishing and reviewing its objectives, an organization shall consider the legal and other requirements, its significant environmental aspects, its technological options and its financial, operational and business requirements, and the views of interested parties.

The objectives and targets shall be consistent with the environmental policy, including the commitment to prevention of pollution.

5. Environmental prorgamme for the site

The company shall establish and maintain a programme for achieving the objectives at the site. It shall include:

a) designation of responsibility for objectives at each function and level of the company;

b) the means by which they are to be achieved.

4.3.4 Environmental management programme(s)

The organization shall establish and maintain (a) programme(s) for achieving its objectives and targets. It shall include

(a) designation of responsibility for achieving objectives and targets at each relevant function and level of the organization;

(b) the means and time-frame by which they are to be achieved.

If a project relates to new developments, and new or modified activities, products or services, programme(s) shall be amended where relevant to ensure that environmental management applies to such projects.

Separate programmes shall be established in respect of the environmental management of projects relating to new developments, or to new or modified products, services or processes, to define:

1. the environmental objectives to be attained;

2. the mechanisms for their achievement;

3. the procedures for dealing with changes and modifications as projects proceed;

4. the corrective mechanisms which shall be employed should the need arise, how they shall be activated and how their adequacy shall be measured in any particular situation in which they are applied.

B. Environmental management systems

The environmental management system shall be designed, implemented and maintained in such a way as to ensure the fulfillment of the requirements defined below.

1. Environmental policy, objectives and programmes

The establishment and periodical reviews, and revision as appropriate, of the company's environmental policy, objectives and programmes for the site, at the highest appropriate management level.

See:

4.2 Policy

4.3.3 Objectives and targets

4.3.4 Environmental management programme(s)

2. Organization and personnel

Responsibility and authority—
Definition and documentation of
responsibility, authority and interre-
lations of key personnel who manage, perform and monitor work
affecting the environment.

Management representative—
Appointment of a management representative having authority and
responsibility for ensuring that the
management system is implemented
and maintained.

Personnel, communication and training—Ensuring among personnel, at
all levels, awareness of:

a) the importance of compliance
with the environmental policy and
objectives, and with the requirements applicable under the management system established;

b) the potential environmental
effects of their work activities and
the environmental benefits of
improved performance;

c) their roles and responsibilities in
achieving compliance with the environmental policy and objectives, and
with the requirements of the management system;

d) the potential consequences of
departure from the agreed operating
procedures;

Identifying training needs and providing appropriate training for all
personnel whose work may have a
significant effect upon the environment.

4.4.1 Structure and responsibility

Roles, responsibility and authorities
shall be defined, documented and
communicated in order to facilitate
effective environmental management.

Management shall provide resources
essential to the implementation and
control of the environmental management system. Resources include
human resources and specialized
skills, technology and financial
resources.

The organization's top management
shall appoint (a) specific management representative(s) who, irrespective of other responsibilities,
shall have defined roles, responsibilities and authority for

a) ensuring that environmental
management system requirements
are established, implemented and
maintained in accordance with this
International Standard;

b) reporting on the performance of
the environmental management system to top management for review
and as a basis for improvement of
the environmental management
system.

4.4.2 Training, awareness and competence

The organization shall identify training needs. It shall require that all
personnel whose work may create a
significant impact upon the environment, have received appropriate
training.

It shall establish and maintain
procedures to make its employees
or members at each relevant level
aware of

The company shall establish and maintain procedures for receiving, documenting and responding to communications (internal and external) from relevant interested parties concerning its environmental effects and management.

a) the importance of conformance with the environmental policy and procedures and with the requirements of the environmental management system;

b) the significant environmental impacts, actual or potential, of their work activities and the environmental benefits of improved personal performance;

c) their roles and responsibilities in achieving conformance with the environmental policy and procedures and with the requirements of the environmental management system, including emergency preparedness and response requirements;

d) the potential consequences of departure from specified operating procedures.

Personnel performing the tasks which can cause significant environmental impacts shall be competent on the basis of appropriate education, training and/or experience.

4.4.3 Communication

With regard to its environmental aspects and environmental management system, the organization shall establish and maintain procedures for

a) internal communication between the various levels and functions of the organization;

b) receiving, documenting and responding to relevant communication from external interested parties.

The organization shall consider processes for external communication on its significant environmental aspects and record its decision.

3. Environmental effects

Environmental effects evaluation and registration—Examining and assessing the environmental effects of company's activities at the site, and compiling a register of those identified as significant. This shall include, where appropriate, consideration of:

a) controlled and uncontrolled emissions to the atmosphere;

b) controlled and uncontrolled discharges to water or sewers;

c) solid and other wastes, particularly hazardous wastes;

d) contamination of land;

e) use of land, water, fuels and energy, and other natural resources;

f) discharge of thermal energy, noise, odour, dust, vibration and visual impact;

g) effects on specific parts of the environment and ecosystems.

This shall include effects arising, or likely to arise, as consequences of:

1. normal operating conditions;

2. abnormal operating conditions;

3. incidents, accidents and potential emergency conditions;

4. past activities, current activities and planned activities.

Register of legislative, regulatory and other policy requirements—The company shall establish and maintain procedures to record all legislative, regulatory and other policy requirements pertaining to the environmental aspects of its activities, products and services.

4.3.1 Environmental aspects

The organization shall establish and maintain (a) procedure(s) to identify the environmental aspects of its activities, products or services that it can control and over which it can be expected to have an influence, in order to determine those which have or can have significant impacts on the environment. The organization shall ensure that the aspects related to these significant impacts are considered in setting its environmental objectives.

The organization shall keep this information up-to-date.

4.3.2 Legal and other requirements

The organization shall establish and maintain a procedure to identify and have access to legal and other requirements to which the organization subscribes, that are applicable to the environmental aspects of its activities, products or services.

4. Operational control

Establishment of operating procedures—Identification of functions, activities and processes which affect or have the potential to affect the environment, and are relevant to the company's policy and objectives.

Planning and control of such functions, activities and processes, and with particular attention to:

a) documented work instructions defining the manner of conducting the activity, whether by the company's own employees or by others acting on its behalf. Such instructions shall be prepared for situations in which the absence of such instructions could result in infringement of the environmental policy;

b) procedures dealing with procurement and contracted activities to ensure that suppliers and those acting on the company's behalf comply with the company's environmental policy as it relates to them;

c) monitoring and control of relevant process characteristics (e.g., effluent streams and waste disposal);

d) approval of planned processes and equipment;

e) criteria for performance, which shall be stipulated in written standards.

4.4.6 Operational control

The organization shall identify those operations and activities that are associated with the identified significant environmental aspects in line with its policy, objectives and targets. The organization shall plan these activities, including maintenance, in order to ensure that they are carried out under specified conditions by

a) establishing and maintaining documented procedures to cover situations where their absence could lead to deviations from the environmental policy and the objectives and targets;

b) stipulating operating criteria in the procedures;

c) establishing and maintaining procedures related to the identifiable significant environmental aspects of goods and services used by the organization and communicating relevant procedures and requirements to suppliers and contractors.

Monitoring—Monitoring by the company of meeting the requirements established by the company's environmental policy, programme and management system for the site; and for establishing and maintaining records of the results. For each relevant activity or area, this implies:

a) identifying and documenting the monitoring information to be obtained;

b) specifying and documenting the monitoring procedures to be used;

c) and documenting acceptance criteria and the action to be taken when results are unsatisfactory;

d) establishing and documenting the validity of previous monitoring information when monitoring systems are found to be malfunctioning.

4.5.1 Monitoring and measurement

The organization shall establish and maintain documented procedures to monitor and measure, on a regular basis, the key characteristics of its operations and activities that can have a significant impact on the environment. This shall include the recording of information to track performance, relevant operational controls and conformance with the organization's objectives and targets.

Monitoring equipment shall be calibrated and maintained and records of this process shall be retained according to the organization's procedures.

The organization shall establish and maintain a documented procedure for periodically evaluating compliance with relevant environmental legislation and regulations.

Non-compliance and corrective action—Investigation and corrective action, in case of non-compliance with the company's environmental policy, objectives or standards, in order to:

a) determine the cause;

b) draw up a plan of action;

c) initiate preventive actions, to a level corresponding to the risks encountered;

d) apply controls to ensure that any preventive actions taken are effective;

e) record any changes in procedures resulting from corrective action.

4.5.2 Nonconformance and corrective and preventive action

The organization shall establish and maintain procedures for defining responsibility and authority for handling and investigating nonconformance, taking action to mitigate any impacts caused and for initiating and completing corrective and preventive action.

Any corrective or preventive action taken to eliminate the causes of actual and potential nonconformances shall be appropriate to the magnitude of problems and commensurate with the environmental impact encountered.

The organization shall implement and record any changes in the documented procedures resulting from corrective and preventive action.

5. Environmental management documentation records Establishing documentation with a view to:

a) present in a comprehensive way the environmental policy, objectives, and programme;

b) document the key roles and responsibilities;

c) describe the interactions of system elements.

4.4.4 Environmental management system documentation

The organization shall establish and maintain information, in paper or electronic form, to

a) describe the core elements of the management system and their interaction;

b) provide direction to related documentation.

Establishing records in order to demonstrate compliance with the requirements of the environmental management system, and to record the extent to which planned environmental objectives have been met.

4.5.3 Records

The organization shall establish and maintain procedures for the identification, maintenance and disposition of environmental records. These records shall include training records and the results of audits and reviews.

Environmental records shall be legible, identifiable and traceable to the activity, product or service involved. Environmental records shall be stored and maintained in such a way that they are readily retrievable and protected against damage, deterioration or loss. Their retention times shall be established and recorded.

Records shall be maintained, as appropriate to the system and to the organization, to demonstrate conformance to the requirements of this International Standard.

4.4.5 Document control

The organization shall establish and maintain procedures for controlling all documents required by this International Standard to ensure that

a) they can be located;

b) they are periodically reviewed, revised as necessary and approved for adequacy by authorized personnel;

c) the current versions of relevant documents are available at all locations where operations essential to the effective functioning of the environmental management system are performed;

d) obsolete documents are promptly removed from all points of issue and points of use, or otherwise assured against unintended use;

e) any obsolete documents retained for legal and/or knowledge preservation purposes are suitably identified.

Documentation shall be legible, dated (with dates of revision) and readily identifiable, maintained in an orderly manner and retained for a specified period. Procedures and responsibilities shall be established and maintained concerning the creation and modification of the various types of document.

6. Environmental audits

Management implementation and review of a systematic and periodical programme concerning:

a) whether or not environmental management activities conform to the environmental programme, and are implemented effectively;

b) the effectiveness of the environmental management system in fulfilling the company's environmental policy.

4.5.4 Environmental management system audit

The organization shall establish and maintain (a) programme(s) and procedures for periodic environmental management system audits to be carried out, in order to

a) determine whether or not the environmental management system

   1) conforms to planned arrangements for environmental management, including the requirements of this International Standard; and

   2) has been properly implemented and maintained; and

b) provide information on the results of audits to management.

The organization's audit programme, including any schedule, shall be based on the environmental importance of the activity concerned and the results of previous audits. In order to be comprehensive, the audit procedures shall cover the audit scope, frequency and methodologies, as well as the responsibilities and requirements for conducting audits and reporting results.

4.6 Management review

The organization's top management shall, at intervals it determines, review the environmental management system to ensure its continuing suitability, adequacy and effectiveness. The management review process shall ensure that the necessary information is collected to allow management to carry out this evaluation. This review shall be documented.

The management review shall address the possible need for changes to policy, objectives and other elements of the environmental management system, in the light of environmental management system audit results, changing circumstances and the commitment to continual improvement.

C. Issues to be covered

Most of these issues not addressed

The following issues shall be addressed within the framework of the environmental policy and pro-grammes and of environmental audits.

4.4.7 Emergency preparedness and response

1. Assessment, control, and reduction of the impact of the activity concerned on the various sectors of the environment.

The organization shall establish and maintain procedures to identify potential for and respond to accidents and emergency situations, and for preventing and mitigating the environmental impacts that may be associated with them.

2. Energy management, savings and choice.

3. Raw materials management, savings, choice and transportation; water management and savings.

The organization shall review and revise, where necessary, its emergency preparedness and response procedures, in particular, after the occurrence of accidents or emergency situations.

4. Waste avoidance, recycling, reuse, transportation and disposal.

5. Evaluation, control and reduction of noise within and outside the site.

The organization shall also periodically test such procedures where practicable.

6. Selection of new production processes and changes to production processes.

7. Product planning (design, packaging, transportation, use and disposal).

8. Environmental performance and practices of contractors, subcontractors and suppliers.

9. Prevention and limitation of environmental accidents.

10. Contingency procedures in cases of environmental accidents.

11. Staff information and training on environmental issues.

12. External information on environmental issues.

D. Good management practices

The company's environmental policy shall be based on the principles of action set out below; the activities of the company shall be checked regularly to see if they are consistent with these principles and that of continual improvement in environmental performance.

1. a sense of responsibility for the environment amongst employees at all levels shall be fostered.

2. The environmental impact of all new activities, products and processes shall be assessed in advance.

3. The impact of current activities on the local environment shall be assessed and monitored, and any significant impact of these activities on the environment in general shall be examined.

4. Measures necessary to prevent or eliminate pollution, and where this is not feasible, to reduce pollutant emissions and waste generation to the minimum and to conserve resources shall be taken, taking account of possible clean technologies.

Not addressed

5. Measures necessary to prevent accidental emissions of materials or energy shall be taken.

6. Monitoring procedures shall be established and applied, to check compliance with the environmental policy and, where these procedures require measurement and testing, to establish and update records of the results.

7. Procedures and action to be pursued in the event of detection of non-compliance with its environmental policy, objectives or targets, shall be established and updated.

8. Cooperation with the public authorities shall be ensured to establish and update contingency procedures to minimize the impact of any accidental discharges to the environment that nevertheless occur.

9. Information necessary to understand the environmental impact of the company's activities shall be provided to the public, and an open dialogue with the public should be pursued.

10. Appropriate advice shall be provided to customers on the relevant environmental aspects of the handling, use and disposal of the products made by the company.

11. Provisions shall be taken to ensure that contractors working at the site on the company's behalf apply environmental standards equivalent to the company's own.

Summary of EMAS/ISO 14001 Comparison

EMAS Annex I vs. ISO 14001		ISO 14001 vs. EMAS Annex I	
A1, A2, A3	4.2	4.2	A1, A2, A3, B1
A4	4.3.3	4.3.1	B3
A5	4.3.4	4.3.2	B3
B1	4.2, 4.3.3, 4.3.4	4.3.3	A4, B1
B2	4.4.1, 4.4.2, 4.4.3	4.3.4	A5, B1
B3	4.3.1, 4.3.2	4.4.1	B2
B4	4.4.6, 4.5.1, 4.5.2	4.4.2	B2
B5	4.4.4, 4.5.3, 4.4.5	4.4.3	B2
B6	4.5.4, 4.6	4.4.4	B5
C	4.4.7	4.4.5	B5
D	N/A	4.4.6	B4
		4.4.7	C (item 10)
		4.5.1	B4
		4.5.2	B4
		4.5.3	B5
		4.5.4	B6
		4.6	B6

Comparison of BS 7750 and EMAS Annex I to ISO 14001

ISO 14001	BS 7750	EMAS ANNEX I
Scope		
Applicable to all types and sizes of organization	**Also** applicable to all types and sizes of organization	Applicable to selected manufacturing companies
Can be implemented company-wide or at specific sites	**Also** can be implemented company-wide or at specific sites	Must be implemented on a site basis
Focus		
Emphasizes environmental management	Emphasizes environmental performance	Emphasizes environmental performance
Does not require initial review; annex (guidance) recommends initial review for organizations that do not have an EMS in place	Does not require initial review; annex (guidance) recommends initial review for organizations that do not have an EMS in place	Requires initial review
Identification of environmental aspects can consider any issues that the company deems significant	Identification of environmental effects must include six specified areas of concern, as appropriate	Identification of environmental effects must include specified areas of concern, as appropriate
Public Reporting		
Does not require annual environmental statement	**Also** does not require annual environmental statement	Requires annual environmental statement and independent verification of that statement

ISO 14001	BS 7750	EMAS ANNEX I
Commitment and Policy		
4.1 Establishes an EMS	4.1 **Also** establishes an EMS But stipulates that it is a means of addressing environmental effects	
4.2 Environmental policy requires commitment to continual improvement, prevention of pollution, and compliance with relevant environmental legislation and regulations; must be available to the public	4.2 **Also** must be available to the public **But** requires commitment to continual improvement of environmental performance; does not reference prevention of pollution or compliance with environmental legislation and regulations; requires indication of how environmental objectives will be made publicly available	A1-3 **Also** requires compliance with relevant regulations; must be available to the public **But** requires continual improvement of environmental performance; does not reference prevention of pollution
Planning		
4.3.1 Identification of environmental aspects with significant impacts that the organization can control	4.4.2 **Also** requires identification and evaluation of environmental effects **But** requires identification of direct and indirect effects and compilation of a register of those effects that are significant	B3 **Also** requires assessment of environmental effects **But** assessment is done for activities at a site; requires compilation of a register of significant environmental effects

ISO 14001	BS 7750	EMAS ANNEX I
4.3.2 Identification of and access to legal and other requirements	4.4.3 **Also** requires identification of applicable legislative, regulatory, and other policy requirements and codes **But** requirements and codes must be recorded	B3 **Also** requires identification of legislative, regulatory, and other policy requirements pertaining to environmental aspects **But** requirements must be recorded in a register
4.3.3 Objectives and targets must be consistent with the environmental policy including the commitment to prevention of pollution	4.5 **Also** requires that objectives and targets shall be consistent with the environmental policy **But** requires that the commitment to continual improvement in environmental performance shall be quantified over a defined time period	A4 **Also** requires that objectives shall be consistent with the environmental policy **But** does not mention targets; requires that the commitment to continual improvement in environmental performance shall be quantified over a defined time period
4.3.4 Program to achieve objectives and targets must designate responsibility, and means and time frame for achievement; program must be modified to accommodate new activities	4.6 **Also** requires that program to achieve objectives and targets must designate responsibility, and means of achievement **But** separate programs must be developed for new activities	A5 **Also** requires that site program to achieve objectives and targets must designate responsibility, and means of achievement **But** separate programs must be developed for new activities

ISO 14001	BS 7750	EMAS ANNEX I
Implementation and Operation		
4.4.1 Roles and responsibilities must be defined; resources must be made available; specific management representative must be appointed	4.3.1 **Also** states that responsibility and authority must be defined; adequate resources and personnel must be provided **But** requires verification procedures (4.3.2) 4.3.3 **Also** stipulates that specific management representative must be appointed	B2 **Also** requires that roles and responsibilities must be defined; resources must be made available; specific management representative must be appointed
4.4.2 Training needs must be identified; training must be provided to all personnel whose work can impact the environment	4.3.4 **Also** requires that training needs must be identified; training must be provided to all personnel whose work can impact the environment	B2 **Also** requires that training needs must be identified; training must be provided to all personnel whose work can impact the environment
4.4.3 Procedure for communicating internally; procedure for receiving, documenting and responding to relevant interested parties regarding environmental aspects and the EMS; processes for external communication on significant environmental aspects must be considered and a decision recorded	4.4.1 **Also** requires procedure for receiving, documenting and responding to relevant interested parties concerning environmental effects and management **But** does not reference procedure for internal communication	B2 **Also** requires procedure for receiving, documenting and responding to relevant interested parties concerning environmental effects and management **But** does not reference procedure for internal communication

ISO 14001	BS 7750	EMAS ANNEX I
4.4.4 Paper or electronic description of the EMS and direction to related documentation	4.7.1 **Also** permits paper or electronic format; requires direction to related documentation **But** specifies manual with collation of policy, objectives and targets, and program, roles and responsibilities	B5 **Also** requires comprehensive presentation **But** specifies inclusion of the policy, objectives, program, roles and responsibilities, and interactions of key elements; does not address paper versus electronic format
4.4.5 Procedures for controlling all documents to ensure availability of current documents, removal of obsolete documents	4.7.1 **Also** requires procedures for controlling all documents to ensure availability of current documents, removal of obsolete documents	(no comparable requirement)
4.4.6 Identification of operations and activities associated with significant environmental aspects; planning to ensure they are carried out under specified conditions	4.8.2 **Also** requires identification of functions, activities and processes which affect the environment; planning to ensure they are carried out under specified conditions	B4 **Also** requires identification of functions, activities and processes which affect the environment; planning to ensure they are carried out under specified conditions
4.4.7 Procedures to identify potential for and respond to accidents and emergency situations and for preventing or mitigating associated environmental impacts	(no comparable requirement)	C9 **Also** requires prevention and limitation of environmental accidents; and C10 Contingency procedures in cases of environmental accidents (shall be addressed within the framework of the policy and programs and environmental audits

ISO 14001	BS 7750	EMAS ANNEX I
Checking and Corrective Action		
4.5.1 Monitor and measure key characteristics of activities that have a significant impact on the environment; calibrate monitoring equipment; establish a procedure for evaluating regulatory compliance; maintain records of results	4.8.3 **Also** requires procedure to verify compliance with specified requirements; calibration procedure **But** does not reference procedure for evaluating regulatory compliance	B4 **Also** mandates monitoring of requirements established by the policy, program and management system for the site **But** does not reference procedures for calibration or evaluating regulatory compliance
4.5.2 Define responsibility and authority for handling and investigating nonconformance and for initiating and completing corrective and preventive action	4.8.4 **Also** defines responsibility and authority for initiating investigation and corrective action	B4 **Also** requires investigation and corrective action in case of noncompliance with the company's policy, objectives or standards
4.5.3 Procedure to identify, maintain and dispose of environmental records, including training records and the results of audits and reviews	4.9 **Also** requires system of records to demonstrate compliance with the requirements of the EMS, including training records and the results of audits and reviews **But** specifies contractor and procurement records	B5 **Also** requires records to demonstrate compliance with the requirements of the EMS and the extent to which planned environmental objectives have been met **But** does not specify what records must be included

ISO 14001	BS 7750	EMAS ANNEX I
4.5.4 Periodic EMS audits to determine whether the EMS conforms to this standard and has been properly implemented and maintained	4.10.1 **Also** establishes an audit program to determine whether environmental management activities conform to planned requirements and are effective in fulfilling the environmental policy	B6 **Also** requires periodic audits to determine whether environmental management activities conform to the environmental program and are implemented effectively, and the effectiveness of the EMS in fulfilling the environmental policy
Management Review 4.6 Periodic review by top management to ensure continuing suitability, adequacy and effectiveness of the EMS	4.11 **Also** requires periodic review by management to ensure continuing suitability and effectiveness of the EMS	(no comparable requirement)

Comparison of NSF 110 and ISO 14001

NSF 110

3.1 Policy

3.1.1 Senior management shall define and maintain an environmental policy that is relevant to the nature, scale, and environmental effects of its activities, products, and services.

3.1.2 An organization's environmental policy shall include a commitment to the establishment, maintenance, and continuous improvement of an EMS.

3.1.3 An organization's environmental policy shall include a commitment to comply with relevant environmental legislation and regulations.

3.1.4 An organization's environmental policy shall take onto account the relevant provisions of its own internal corporate standards and guidelines as well as the relevant requirements of other voluntary programs to which it subscribes.

3.1.5 An organization's environmental policy shall be distributed throughout the organization and shall be made available to the public.

ISO 14001

4.2 Environmental policy

Top management shall define the organization's environmental policy and ensure that it

a) is appropriate to the nature, scale and environmental impacts of its activities, products, or services;

b) includes a commitment to continual improvement and prevention of pollution;

c) includes a commitment to comply with relevant environmental legislation and regulations, and with other requirements to which the organization subscribes;

d) provides the framework for setting and reviewing environmental objectives and targets;

e) is documented, implemented and maintained and communicated to all employees;

f) is available to the public.

NSF 110-1995 reprinted with permission from NSF International, Ann Arbor, Michigan.

Reprinted with permission from ASQC, Milwaukee, Wisconsin.

3.2 Organization and personnel

3.2.1 Management shall provide resources and personnel essential to the effective implementation and verification of the EMS.

3.2.2 The responsibility and accountability for functions related to environmental management shall be clearly defined and documented in relation to the structure of the organization.

3.2.3 Environmental management functions shall be integrated into other management and organizational functions, as appropriate, to support the attainment of the stated environmental management objectives and targets.

3.2.4 Personnel with environmental management responsibilities shall have the authority necessary to effectively carry out those responsibilities. The organizational structure shall accurately reflect the authority and reporting relationships of personnel engaged in environmental management functions.

3.2.5 The appropriate environmental management responsibilities shall be specified in the job descriptions for all positions involved in environmental management functions.

3.2.6 Environmental performance shall be integrated into the performance appraisal process for appropriate employees.

4.4.1 Structure and responsibility

Roles, responsibility and authorities shall be defined, documented and communicated in order to facilitate effective environmental management.

Management shall provide resources essential to the implementation and control of the environmental management system. Resources include human resources and specialized skills, technology and financial resources.

The organization's top management shall appoint (a) specific management representative(s) who, irrespective of other responsibilities, shall have defined roles, responsibilities and authority for

a) ensuring that environmental management system requirements are established, implemented and maintained in accordance with this International Standard;

b) reporting on the performance of the environmental management system to top management for review and as a basis for improvement of the environmental management system.

3.2.7 Personnel with specific environmental management responsibilities shall have the knowledge, skills, and training necessary to adequately fulfill those responsibilities.

3.2.8 An organization shall establish procedures for identifying training needs and for providing the appropriate training for employees in areas related to the environment and environmental management. Training received shall be appropriate to the job function and shall be updated periodically.

4.4.2 Training, awareness and competence

The organization shall identify training needs. It shall require that all personnel whose work may create a significant impact upon the environment, have received appropriate training.

It shall establish and maintain procedures to make its employees or members at each relevant function and level aware of

a) the importance of conformance with the environmental policy and procedures and with the requirements of the environmental management system;

b) the significant environmental impacts, actual or potential, of their work activities and the environmental benefits of improved personal performance;

c) their roles and responsibilities in achieving conformance with the environmental policy and procedures and with the requirements of the environmental management system, including emergency preparedness and response requirements;

d) the potential consequences of departure from specified operating procedures.

Personnel performing the tasks which can cause significant environmental impacts shall be competent on the basis of appropriate education, training and/or experience.

3.3 Environmental objectives and targets

3.3.1 An organization shall adopt a process for evaluating the significant environmental effects of its activities, products, and services, consistent with scientific understanding of environmental effects and generally-accepted assessment methodologies. The nature and scope of these assessments, as well as the priorities for conducting them, shall be established in consideration of the significance of potential health risks or environmental risks, or both; business considerations; previous incidents; the extent to which an organization has control over effects; and public interest. Results of assessments hall be reviewed periodically, based on new information or improvements in methodology.

3.3.2 An organization shall identify legislative, regulatory, and other requirements that are directly applicable to the environmental effects of its activities, products, and services.

3.3.3 An organization shall identify and evaluate the interests and expectations of key stakeholders in the activities of the organization.

4.3.1 Environmental aspects

The organization shall establish and maintain (a) procedure(s) to identify the environmental aspects of its activities, products or services that it can control and over which it can be expected to have an influence, in order to determine those which have or can have significant impacts on the environment. The organization shall ensure that the aspects related to these significant impacts are considered in setting its environmental objectives.

The organization shall keep this information up-to-date.

4.3.2 Legal and other requirements

The organization shall establish and maintain a procedure to identify and have access to legal and other requirements to which the organization subscribes, that are applicable to the environmental aspects of its activities, products or services.

3.3.4 An organization shall define its environmental objectives and corresponding environmental targets. Objectives and targets shall be developed with consideration of the following:

—the organization's environmental policy;

—the evaluation conducted in accordance with 3.3.1, 3.3.2, and 3.3.3 of this standard; and

—the financial, operational, and business requirements of the organization.

3.3.5 The environmental objectives and targets shall be considered in the development of the appropriate plans and budgets throughout the organization.

4.3.3 Objectives and targets

The organization shall establish and maintain documented environmental objectives and targets, at each relevant function and level within the organization.

When establishing and reviewing its objectives, an organization shall consider the relevant legal and other requirements, its significant environmental aspects, its technological options, and its financial, operational and business requirements, and the views of interested parties.

The objectives and targets shall be consistent with the environmental policy, including the commitment to prevention of pollution.

3.4 Program implementation

3.4.1 An organization shall implement specific management programs to achieve it environmental objectives and targets and to ensure that the level of environmental performance is consistent with the organization's environmental policy. Programs shall:

—designate responsibility for achieving targets for each relevant function and at each level of the organization, and

—specify the means and timeframe by which targets are to be achieved.

3.4.2 When necessary, environmental programs shall be amended to account for changes associated with new or modified activities, products, and services.

3.5 Control procedures for routine operations

An organization shall establish and document procedures for monitoring and controlling operations and activities (identified in 3.3.1) in a manner consistent with the organization's environmental policy. Legal requirements, objectives, and targets.

4.3.4 Environmental management programme(s)

The organization shall establish and maintain (a) programme(s) for achieving its objectives and targets. It shall include

(a) designation of responsibility for achieving objectives and targets at each relevant function and level of the organization;

(b) the means and time-frame by which they are to be achieved.

If a project relates to new developments, and new or modified activities, products or services, programme(s) shall be amended where relevant to ensure that environmental management applies to such projects.

4.4.6 Operational control

The organization shall identify those operations and activities that are associated with the identified significant environmental aspects in line with its policy, objectives and targets. The organization shall plan these activities, including maintenance, in order to ensure that they are carried out under specified conditions by

a) establishing and maintaining documented procedures to cover situations where their absence could lead to deviations from the environmental policy and the objectives and targets;

b) stipulating operating criteria in the procedures;

c) establishing and maintaining procedures related to the identifiable significant environmental aspects of goods and services used by the organization and communicating relevant procedures and requirements to suppliers and contractors.

3.6 Emergency preparedness and response

An organization shall develop and implement a plan for effective emergency preparedness and response. The plan shall identify the hazards associates with the activities of an organization. It shall also identify the resources, personnel, training, testing, communication, and appropriate lines of authority required to effectively respond to and mitigate an emergency.

4.4.7 Emergency preparedness and response

The organization shall establish and maintain procedures to identify potential for and respond to accidents and emergency situations, and for preventing and mitigating the environmental impacts that may be associated with them.

The organization shall review and revise, where necessary, its emergency preparedness and response procedures, in particular, after the occurrence of accidents or emergency situations.

The organization shall also periodically test such procedures where practicable.

3.7 Verification and review

3.7.1 An organization shall establish and maintain a program to plan and carry out periodic environmental audits.

4.5.4 Environmental management system audit

The organization shall establish and maintain (a) programme(s) and procedures for periodic environmental management system audits to be carried out, in order to

a) determine whether or not the environmental management system

1) conforms to planned arrangements for environmental management including the requirements of this International Standard; and

2) has been properly implemented and maintained; and

b) provide information on the results of audits to management.

The organization's audit programme, including any schedule, shall be based on the environmental importance of the activity concerned and the results of previous audits. In order to be comprehensive, the audit procedures shall cover the audit scope, frequency and methodologies, as well as the responsibilities and requirements for conducting audits and reporting results.

3.7.2 An organization shall periodically conduct a management review to determine the adequacy of its EMS in fulfilling the organization's environmental policy.

4.6 Management review

The organization's top management shall, at intervals it determines, review the environmental management system, to ensure its continuing suitability, adequacy and effectiveness. The management review process shall ensure that the necessary information is collected to allow management to carry out this evaluation. This review shall be documented.

The management review shall address the possible need for changes to policy, objectives and other elements of the environmental management system, in the light of environmental management system audit results, changing circumstances and the commitment to continual improvement.

3.7.3 An organization shall

—identify appropriate measures of environmental performance;

—monitor, track, and evaluate environmental performance results against established environmental objectives and targets; and

—implement and track corrective action plans.

4.5.1 Monitoring and measurement

The organization shall establish and maintain documented procedures to monitor and measure, on a regular basis, the key characteristics of its operations and activities that can have a significant impact on the environment. This shall include the recording of information to track performance, relevant operational controls and conformance with the organization's objectives and targets.

Monitoring equipment shall be calibrated and maintained and records of this process shall be retained according to the organization's procedures.

The organization shall establish and maintain a documented procedure for periodically evaluating compliance with relevant environmental legislation and regulations.

4.5.2 Nonconformance and corrective and preventive action

The organization shall establish and maintain procedures for defining responsibility and authority for handling and investigating nonconformance, taking action to mitigate any impacts caused and for initiating and completing corrective and preventive action.

Any corrective or preventive action taken to eliminate the causes of actual and potential nonconformances shall be appropriate to the magnitude of problems and commensurate with the environmental impact encountered.

The organization shall implement and record any changes in the documented procedures resulting from corrective and preventive action.

3.8 Documentation

3.8.1 An organization shall establish and maintain procedures for managing all documents necessary to implement and maintain an EMS. The procedure shall ensure that documents

—can be identified with the appropriate place in the organization;

—are periodically reviewed, revised as necessary, and approved for adequacy by authorized personnel prior to issue;

—are available in their current version at all locations where operations essential to the effective functioning of the system are performed; and

—when obsolete, are clearly marked as such or are promptly removed from all points of issue and points of use.

3.8.2 Documentation in written or electronic form shall be legible, dated with dates of revisions), readily identifiable, maintained in an orderly manner, and retained for a specified period. Clear policies and responsibilities shall be established concerning the modification of documents.

4.4.4 Environmental management system documentation

The organization shall establish and maintain information, in paper or electronic form, to

a) describe the core elements of the management system and their interaction;

b) provide direction to related documentation.

4.4.5 Document control

The organization shall establish and maintain procedures for controlling all documents required by this International Standard to ensure that

a) they can be located;

b) they are periodically reviewed, revised as necessary and approved for adequacy by authorized personnel;

c) the current versions of relevant documents are available at all locations where operations essential to the effective functioning of the environmental management system are performed;

d) obsolete documents are promptly removed from all points of issue and points of use, or otherwise assured against unintended use;

e) any obsolete documents retained for legal and/or knowledge preservation purposes are suitably identified.

Documentation shall be legible, dated (with dates of revision), and readily identifiable, maintained in an orderly manner and retained for a specified period. Procedures and responsibilities shall be established and maintained concerning the creation and modification of the various types of document.

3.9 Communications

3.9.1 An organization shall establish procedures for the regular internal communication of findings, conclusions, and recommendations derived from environment effects assessments, environmental audits, environmental performance evaluations, and management review. Communications procedures shall ensure that the appropriate management personnel and those directly responsible for taking action are routinely and fully informed of relevant environmental matters.

3.9.2 An organization shall establish and implement procedures for communicating with external stakeholders on environmental matters.

4.4.3 Communication

With regard to its environmental aspects and environmental management system, the organization shall establish and maintain procedures for

a) internal communication between the various levels and functions of the organization;

b) receiving, documenting and responding to relevant communication from external interested parties.

The organization shall consider processes for external communication on its significant environmental aspects and record its decision.

Comparison of the ICC Business Charter for Sustainable Development and ISO 14001

The Business Charter for Sustainable Development was published by the International Chamber of Commerce for distribution at the 1991 Second World Industry Conference on Environmental Management. Its 16 principles are intended to help businesses throughout the world improve their environmental performance and contribute to sustainable development.

Business Charter Principles	ISO 14001
1. Corporate priority To recognize environmental management as among the highest corporate priorities and as a key determinant to sustainable development; to establish policies, programs and practices for conducting operations in an environmentally sound manner.	4.2 Environmental policy 4.3.4 Environmental management programme(s)
2. Integrated management To integrate these policies, programs and practices fully into each business as an essential element of management in all its functions.	4.4.1 Structure and responsibility
3. Process of improvement To continue to improve corporate policies, programs and environmental performance, taking into account technical developments, scientific understanding, consumer needs and community expectations, with legal regulations as a starting point; and to apply the same environmental criteria internationally.	4.3.2 Legal and other requirements

The Business Charter for Sustainable Development—Principles for Environmental Management, 1991, reprinted with permission from International Chamber of Commerce, Paris, France.

4. Employee education To educate, train and motivate employees to conduct their activities in an environmentally responsible manner.	4.4.2 Training, awareness and competence
5. Prior assessment To assess environmental impacts before starting a new activity or project and before decommissioning a facility or leaving a site.	4.3.1 Environmental aspects
6. Products and services To develop and provide products or services that have no undue environmental impact and are safe in their intended use, that are efficient in their consumption of energy and natural resources, and that can be recycled, reused, or disposed of safely.	4.3.3 Objectives and targets
7. Customer advice To advise, and where relevant educate, customers, distributors and the public in the safe use, transportation, storage and disposal of products provided; and to apply similar considerations to the provision of services.	4.4.3 Communication
8. Facilities and operations To develop, design and operate facilities and conduct activities taking into consideration the efficient use of energy and materials, the sustainable use of renewable resources, the minimization of adverse environmental impact and waste generation, and the safe and responsible disposal of residual wastes.	4.4.6 Operational control
9. Research To conduct or support research on the environmental impacts of raw materials, products, processes, emissions and wastes associated with the enterprise and on the means of minimizing such adverse impacts.	4.3.1 Environmental aspects

10. Precautionary approach
To modify the manufacture, marketing or use of products or services or the conduct of activities, consistent with scientific and technical understanding, to prevent serious or irreversible environmental degradation.

11. Contractors and suppliers To promote the adoption of these principles by contractors acting on behalf of the enterprise, encouraging and, where appropriate, requiring improvements in their practices to make them consistent with those of the enterprise; and to encourage the wider adoption of these principles by suppliers.	4.4.6 Operational control—section c
12. Emergency preparedness To develop and maintain, where significant hazards exist, emergency preparedness plans in conjunction with the emergency services, relevant authorities and the local community, recognizing potential transboundary impacts.	4.4.7 Emergency preparedness and response

13. Transfer of technology
To contribute to the transfer of environmentally sound technology and management methods throughout the industrial and public sectors.

14. Contributing to the common effort
To contribute to the development of public policy and to business, governmental and intergovernmental programs and educational initiatives that will enhance environmental awareness and protection.

15. Openness to concerns
To foster openness and dialogue with employees and the public, anticipating and responding to their concerns about the potential hazards and impacts of operations, products, wastes or services, including those of transboundary or global significance.

4.4.3 Communication

16. Compliance and reporting
To measure environmental performance; to conduct regular environmental audits and assessments of compliance with company requirements, legal requirements and these principles; and periodically to provide appropriate information to the Board of Directors, shareholders, employees, the authorities and the public.

4.4.4 EMS documentation

4.5.1 Monitoring and measurement

4.5.2 Nonconformance and corrective and preventive action

4.5.4 EMS audit

4.6 Management review

Comparison of API-STEP and ISO 14001

API-STEP	ISO 14001
Pollution Prevention	
2.3.1 Provide management support for ongoing pollution prevention activities through appropriate policies, actions, communications and resource commitments.	4.3.4 Environmental management programme(s)
2.3.2 Develop and implement a program to improve prevention and early detection and reduce impacts of spills of crude oil and petroleum products and other accidental releases from operations.	4.5.2 Nonconformance and corrective and preventive action
2.3.3 Develop an inventory of significant releases to air, water and land; identify their sources; and evaluate their impact on human health and the environment.	4.3.1 Environmental aspects
2.3.4 Periodically review and identify pollution prevention options and opportunities, develop approaches for reducing releases, and set goals and timing for reducing releases . . .	4.3.3 Objectives and targets
2.3.5 Include pollution prevention objectives in research efforts and in the design of new or modified operations, processes, and products.	4.4.6 Operational control
2.3.6 Support an outreach program to promote pollution prevention opportunities within the industry, including sharing of industry experiences and accomplishments.	4.4.3 Communication

Strategies for Today's Environmental Partnership, 1993, American Petroleum Institute. Reprinted with permission.

Operating and Process Safety

3.3.1 Demonstrate management leadership and support through appropriate policy, communication, and resource commitment for continuous improvement of operational and process safety performance	4.2 Environmental policy 4.3.4 Environmental management programme(s)
3.3.2 Assess, prioritize, and address the environmental, health and safety impacts of our operations.	4.3.1 Environmental aspects 4.3.2 Legal and other requirements
3.3.3 Establish programs, procedures, training, and work practices appropriate to each operation to foster safe, healthful, and environmentally-sound work environments.	4.4.1 Structure and responsibility
3.3.4 Employ processes to select safe contractors, clarify responsibilities, assess performance and exchange information to promote safe work environments.	4.4.2 Training, awareness and competence
3.3.5 Use sound engineering, operating, and maintenance practices consistent with recognized codes and standards in the design, construction, use and maintenance of operations.	4.3.2 Legal and other requirements 4.4.6 Operational control
3.3.6 Document process design, operating parameters and procedures, and other information relating to the hazards of materials and process technology.	4.4.5 Document control 4.5.3 Records
3.3.7 Employ processes to provide for safe transport of raw materials, petroleum products, wastes, and hazardous materials, including selection of reliable carriers and distributors.	4.4.6 Operational control

3.3.8 Investigate and take appropriate action on each incident that results or could have resulted in a significant injury, illness, fire, explosion or accidental release.	4.5.2 Nonconformance and corrective and preventive action
3.3.9 Employ processes to assure that personnel are able to perform their jobs safely and are not compromised by external influences, such as drugs and alcohol.	4.4.2 Training, awareness and competence 4.5.1 Monitoring and measurement
3.3.10 Conduct job safety and occupational health assessments to evaluate risks to personnel from processes, equipment, hazardous materials, and from other work-site conditions.	N/A—ISO 14001 does not address health and safety issues
3.3.11 Manage changes in operations to maintain or enhance the levels of safety and environmental protection designed into those operations.	4.5.1 Monitoring and measurement
3.3.12 Develop processes that assess safety and occupational health management systems.	N/A—ISO 14001 does not address health and safety issues
Community Awareness	
4.3.1 Demonstrate management commitment and leadership aimed at achieving community awareness.	4.2 Environmental policy
4.3.2 Provide an awareness program for employees and contractors that includes periodic assessments of their questions and concerns about the operations.	4.4.2 Training, awareness and competence 4.4.3 Communication
4.3.3 Provide communications training for key company personnel who communicate with employees, contractors, and the public concerning safety, health and environmental issues.	4.4.2 Training, awareness and competence

4.3.4 Provide for education of employees and contractors about the operation's emergency response plan and safety, health and environmental programs.	4.4.2 Training, awareness and competence
4.3.5 Conduct periodic dialogue with employees and contractors to respond to their questions and concerns and involve them, as appropriate, in community awareness efforts.	4.4.3 Communication
4.3.6 Conduct periodic evaluations of the effectiveness of employee and contractor communication efforts.	4.5.1 Monitoring and measurement 4.6 Management review
4.3.7 Provide an awareness program for the community that includes periodic assessments of community questions and concerns about the operation.	4.4.3 Communication
4.3.8 Maintain programs to educate the community, outside emergency responders, government officials, the media, and other businesses about the operation's emergency response program and its health, safety and environmental protection programs.	4.4.3 Communication
4.3.9 Conduct periodic dialogues with appropriate local citizens to respond to questions and concerns about safety, health and the environment.	4.4.3 Communication
4.3.10 Maintain a policy of openness that is responsive to persons interested in becoming familiar with the operation, its products, and its efforts to protect safety, health and the environment.	4.4.3 Communication
4.3.11 Conduct periodic evaluations of the effectiveness of community communication efforts.	4.5.1 Monitoring and measurement 4.6 Management review

Crisis Readiness

5.3.1 Periodically update assessments of potential hazards to employees, local communities, and the environment from accidents or emergencies.	4.4.7 Emergency preparedness and response
5.3.2 Establish, implement, and periodically update emergency response plans and capabilities . . .	4.4.7 Emergency preparedness and response
5.3.3 Develop and use formal procedures for handling prompt and comprehensive communication to employees, government agencies, and the public in the event of a crisis.	4.4.3 Communication 4.4.7 Emergency preparedness and response
5.3.4 Maintain a 24-hour capability for receiving emergency or crisis information and for mobilizing response resources.	4.4.7 Emergency preparedness and response
5.3.5 Conduct employee training programs on a periodic basis for those who have emergency response capabilities.	4.4.2 Training, awareness and competence
5.3.6 Coordinate emergency response plans or investigate community interest in creating a plan if none exists.	4.4.7 Emergency preparedness and response
5.3.7 Incorporate into contingency plans measures to coordinate with government agencies, nearby industry operations, and private community aid organizations for the recovery of communities adversely affected by an operational incident.	4.4.7 Emergency preparedness and response

Product Stewardship

6.3.1 Provide management commitment to product stewardship through appropriate policies, communication and allocation of resources.	4.2 Environmental policy 4.3.4 Environmental management programme(s)
6.3.2 Establish goals and responsibilities for implementing product stewardship activities throughout the organization and periodically measure performance.	4.3.3 Objectives and targets 4.4.1 Structure and responsibility 4.5.1 Monitoring and measurement
6.3.3 Establish and maintain a program to identify and evaluate the health, safety and environmental hazards and exposures related to new and existing products.	4.3.1 Environmental aspects
6.3.4 Develop mechanisms to provide for safe transport of products and selection of reliable transporters.	4.4.6 Operational control
6.3.5 Provide information including emergency procedures to employees, contractors, transporters, distributors, and customers on the safe use, handling, storage, recycling, and disposal of products.	4.4.3 Communication
6.3.6 Establish and implement procedures that consider health, safety, and environmental hazards and exposures in product design, manufacture, distribution, use and disposal.	4.4.6 Operational control

Proactive Government Interaction

7.3.1 Provide information to government and other appropriate parties to foster development of responsible laws, regulations, and standards that reflect benefits, commensurate with costs and recognize technological limitations.	4.4.3 Communication

7.3.2 Identify opportunities to impact current and future government initiatives with sound, reliable information that is scientifically and analytically based.	4.3.1 Environmental aspects
7.3.3 Assure that the development of positions, policy, and supporting information is based on sound and credible principles.	4.4.3 Communication
7.3.4 Assure that advocacy activities are performed in a manner that reflects the highest standards of professional conduct to maintain credibility with government and the public.	4.4.3 Communication
7.3.5 Participate in appropriate cooperative projects to better evaluate innovative ideas.	4.4.3 Communication
7.3.6 Participate in intercompany and industry task forces or industry associations on significant governmental issues.	4.4.3 Communication
Resource Conservation	
8.3.1 Demonstrate management support for energy efficiency and internal conservation efforts through appropriate policy development.	4.2 Environmental policy
8.3.2 Keep employees informed about their role in conserving energy and resource conservation.	4.4.2 Training, awareness and competence 4.4.3 Communication
8.3.3 Improve energy efficiency and resource conservation through facility design, operation, and maintenance.	4.4.6 Operational control
8.3.4 Incorporate improved energy efficiency technologies both in new designs and in retrofits to existing equipment when economically justified.	N/A

8.3.5 Implement procedures to ensure that energy efficiency and resource conservation are considerations in the planning and development of new and substantially modified products and operations.

4.3.1 Environmental aspects

Comparison of ATMI E3 Program and ISO 14001

E3 Program	ISO 14001
1. Attach your company's environmental policy. Model policies are available from ATMI.	4.2 Environmental policy
2. Describe senior management's contribution toward environmental excellence and how greater environmental awareness is encouraged. Commitment to the environment goes beyond words to action. For example, does your company have a formal environmental department with clear responsibilities for dealing with environmental matters? Does your company publish an employee handout or special newsletter section on environmental issues?	4.3.4 Environmental management programme(s) 4.4.1 Structure and responsibility 4.4.3 Communication
3. Attach a copy of your company's audit form. Environmental audits provide companies with an opportunity to ensure their officers and employees that they are in full compliance with existing federal, state and local environmental laws and regulations. For example, who is involved in developing your audit program? How often are audits undertaken? Are audits conducted at every company facility and with whom are audit reports shared?	4.3.2 Legal and other requirements 4.5.1 Monitoring and measurement

Reprinted with permission from American Textile Manufacturers Institute, Washington, D.C.

4. Describe how your company has worked with suppliers as well as customers to address these concerns. Environmental concerns often arise from outside a company. For example, has your company instituted a solid-waste reduction program and worked with suppliers to reduce and/or recycle product packaging? Has your company approached a supplier regarding incorporating new, more efficient and economic water treatment equipment?	4.4.6 Operational control
5. Establish and list your company's environmental goals and targeted achievement dates. Goals can be developed using information gained through environmental audits. For example, reduce the amount of toxic pollutants emitted into the water (as defined under the Superfund Amendments and Reauthorization Act [SARA] Section 313) by 10 percent by 1995, or reduce the amount of solid waste sent to landfills by 15 percent by 1996.	4.3.3 Objectives and targets
6. Describe your company's employee education program. Employees must be aware of a company's environmental policies and concerns to protect their own health and safety as well as to ensure a company's environmental compliance in its day-to-day operations. For example, does your company have a formal environmental education program and must every employee attend? Is your company open to employee suggestions about how to minimize environmental concerns?	4.4.2 Training, awareness and competence

7. Identify and describe your company's emergency response plans, both formal (e.g., spill control and containment plans) and informal (e.g., plant manager's accident plan). Attach copies of your plans. Does your company ever undertake practice drills of such plans to ensure easy and safe implementation?	4.4.7 Emergency preparedness and response
8. How has your company relayed its environmental interests and concerns to your community, its residents and policymakers? Textile companies have been historically closely tied to the communities in which they operate. With the increased focus on environmental issues by the general public and policymakers, this relationship is more important than ever. For example, does your company sponsor plant tours for citizens as well as visitors? Do company representatives meet regularly with local policymakers to discuss environmental concerns?	4.4.3 Communication

9. Describe how your company has been able to offer its environmental assistance and insights to others within your community to citizens, interest groups, other companies, policymakers, etc. Sharing information on wastewater treatment with other companies at trade and business meetings, and organizing a community recycling center with a local school or community group are examples.	4.4.3 Communication
10. Describe your company's interaction with federal, state and local policymakers. For example, is your company represented and actively involved in ATMI's Environmental Preservation Committee? Does your company meet regularly with policymakers regarding proposed environmental policies that would affect companies other than just your own?	4.4.3 Communication

Comparison of CMA Responsible Care®
and ISO 14001

Responsible Care®

ISO 14001

Pollution Prevention

1. A clear commitment by senior management through policy, communications, and resources, to ongoing reductions at each of the company's facilities, in releases to the air, water and land and in the generation of wastes.

4.2 Environmental policy

4.4.1 Structure and responsibility

2. A quantitative inventory at each facility of wastes generated and releases to the air, water, and land, measured or estimated at the point of generation or release.

4.3.1 Environmental aspects

3. Evaluation, sufficient to assist in establishing reduction priorities, of the potential impact of releases on the environment and the health and safety of employees and the public.

4.3.1 Environmental aspects

4. Education of and dialogue with employees and members of the public about the inventory, impact evaluation, and risks to the community.

4.4.3 Communication

5. Establishment of priorities, goals, and plans for waste and release reduction, taking into account both community concerns and the potential health, safety, and environmental impacts as determined under Practices 3 and 4.

4.3.3 Objectives and targets

Chemical Manufacturers Association, 1992.
Reprinted with permission.

6. Ongoing reduction of wastes and releases, giving preference first to source reduction, second to recycle/reuse, and third to treatment.	4.5.1 Monitoring and measurement 4.6 Management review
7. Measurement of progress at each facility in reducing the generation of wastes and in reducing releases to the air, water and land, by updating the quantitative inventory at least annually.	4.3.1 Environmental aspects 4.5.1 Monitoring and measurement
8. Ongoing dialogue with employees and members of the public regarding waste and release information, progress in achieving reductions, and future plans.	4.4.2 Training, awareness and competence 4.4.3 Communication
9. Inclusion of waste and release prevention objectives in research and in the design of new or modified facilities, processes, and products.	4.4.6 Operational control
10. An ongoing program for promotion and support of waste and release reduction by others.	4.4.3 Communication
11. Periodic evaluation of waste management practices associated with operations and equipment at each member company facility, taking into account community concerns and health, safety and environmental impacts, and implementation of ongoing improvements.	4.6 Management review
12. Implementation of a process for selecting, retaining and reviewing contractors and toll manufacturers taking into account sound waste management practices that protect the environment and the health and safety of employees and the public.	N/A
13.Implementation of engineering and operating controls at each member company facility to improve prevention of and early detection of releases that may contaminate groundwater.	4.4.6 Operational control 4.5.2 Nonconformance and corrective and preventive action

14. Implementation of an ongoing program for addressing past operating and waste management practices and for working with others to resolve identified problems at each active or inactive facility owned by a member company taking into account community concerns and health, safety and environmental impacts.	4.3.4 Environmental management programme(s)

Community Awareness and Outreach

For employees:	4.4.2 Training, awareness and competence
1. An ongoing assessment of employee questions and concerns about the facility.	
2. Communications training for key facility and company personnel who communicate with employees and the public concerning safety, health and environmental issues.	4.4.2 Training, awareness and competence
3. Education of employees about the facility's emergency response plan and safety, health and environmental programs	4.4.2 Training, awareness and competence
4. An ongoing dialogue with employees to respond to their questions and concerns and involve them in community outreach efforts.	4.4.3 Communication
5. A regular evaluation of the effectiveness of the ongoing employee communications efforts.	4.5.1 Monitoring and measurement
For the community:	
6. An ongoing assessment of community questions and concerns about the facility	4.4.3 Communication

7. An outreach program to educate responders, government officials, the media, other businesses and the community about the facility's emergency response program and risks to the community associated with the facility.	4.3.1 Environmental aspects 4.4.3 Communication
8. A continuing dialogue with local citizens to respond to questions and concerns about safety, health and the environment, and to address other issues of interest to the community.	4.4.3 Communication
9. A policy of openness that provides convenient ways for interested persons to become familiar with the facility, its operations and products, and its efforts to protect safety, health and the environment.	4.4.3 Communication
10. A regular evaluation of the effectiveness of the ongoing community communications efforts.	4.5.1 Monitoring and measurement 4.6 Management review

Emergency Response

1. An ongoing assessment of potential risks to employees and local communities resulting from accidents or other emergencies.	4.3.1 Environmental aspects
2. A current, written facility emergency response plan which addresses, among other things, communications and the recovery needs of the community after an emergency.	4.4.7 Emergency preparedness and response
3. An ongoing training program for those employees who have response or communications responsibilities in the event of an emergency.	4.4.2 Training, awareness and competence
4. Emergency exercises, at least annually, to test operability of the written emergency response plan.	4.4.7 Emergency preparedness and response
5. Communication of relevant and useful emergency response planning information to the Local Emergency Planning Committee.	4.4.7 Emergency preparedness and response

6. Facility tours for emergency responders to promote emergency preparedness and to provide current knowledge of facility operations.	4.4.2 Training, awareness and competence 4.4.6 Operational control
7. Coordination of the written facility emergency response plan with the comprehensive community emergency response plan and other facilities. If no plan exists, the facility should initiate community efforts to create a plan.	4.4.7 Emergency preparedness and response
8. Participation in the community emergency response planning process to develop and periodically test the comprehensive community emergency response plan developed by the Local Emergency Planning Committee.	4.4.7 Emergency preparedness and response
9. Sharing of information and experience relating to emergency response planning, exercises, and the handling of incidents with other facilities in the community.	4.4.3 Communication 4.5.3 Records

Process Safety

Management Leadership:

1. Leadership by senior management through policy, participation, communications and resource commitments in achieving continuous improvement of performance.	4.2 Environmental policy 4.3.4 Environmental management programme(s)
2. Clear accountability for performance against specific goals for continuous improvement.	4.4.1 Structure and responsibility
3. Measurement of performance, audits for compliance, and implementation of corrective actions.	4.5.1 Monitoring and measurement 4.5.2 Nonconformance and corrective and preventive action
4. Investigation, reporting, appropriate corrective action and follow-up of each incident that results or could have resulted in a fire, explosion or accidental chemical release.	4.5.2 Nonconformance and corrective and preventive action

5. Sharing of relevant safety knowledge and lessons learned from such incidents with industry, government and the community.	4.4.3 Communication
6. Use of the Community Awareness and Emergency Response process to assure public comments and concerns are considered in design and implementation of the facility's process safety systems.	N/A
Technology:	
7. Current, complete documentation of process design and operating parameters and procedures.	4.4.6 Operational control
8. Current, complete documentation of information relating to the hazards of materials and process technology.	4.4.5 Document control
9. Periodic assessment and documentation of process hazards, and implementation of actions to minimize risks associated with chemical operations, including the possibility of human error.	4.4.6 Operational control 4.4.7 Emergency preparedness and response
10. Management of changes to chemical operations to maintain or enhance the safety originally designed into the facility.	4.4.6 Operational control
Facilities:	
11. Consideration and mitigation of the potential safety effects of expansions, modifications and new sites on the community, environment and employees.	4.3.1 Environmental aspects
12. Facility design, construction and maintenance using sound engineering practices consistent with recognized codes and standards.	N/A
13. Safety reviews on all new and modified facilities during design and prior to start-up.	N/A

14. Documented maintenance and inspection programs that ensure facility integrity.	N/A
15. Sufficient layers of protection through technology, facilities and employees to prevent escalation from a single failure to a catastrophic event.	4.4.7 Emergency preparedness and response
16. Provision for control of processes and equipment during emergencies resulting from natural events, utility disruptions and other external conditions.	4.4.6 Operational control
Personnel:	
17. Identification of the skills and knowledge necessary to perform each job.	4.4.2 Training, awareness and competence
18. Establishment of procedures and work practices for safe operating and maintenance activities.	4.4.6 Operational control
19. Training for all employees to reach and maintain proficiency in safe work practices and the skills and knowledge necessary to perform their job.	4.4.2 Training, awareness and competence
20. Demonstrations and documentation of skill proficiency prior to assignment to independent work, and periodically thereafter.	4.4.2 Training, awareness and competence
21. Programs designed to assure that employees in safety critical jobs are fit for duty and are not compromised by external influences, including alcohol and drug abuse.	N/A
22. Provisions that contractors either have programs for their own employees consistent with applicable sections of this Code or be included in the member company's program, or some combination of the two.	N/A

Product Stewardship

1. Leadership: Demonstrates senior management leadership through written policy, active participation and communication.	4.2 Environmental policy 4.4.3 Communication
2. Accountability and performance measurement: Establishes goals and responsibilities for implementing product stewardship throughout the organization. Measures performance against these goals.	4.3.3 Objectives and targets 4.4.1 Structure and responsibility 4.5.1 Monitoring and measurement
3. Resources: Commits resources necessary to implement and maintain product stewardship practices.	4.3.4 Environmental management programme(s)
4. Health, safety and environmental information: Establishes and maintains information on health, safety, and environmental hazards and reasonably foreseeable exposures from new and existing products.	4.3.1 Environmental aspects 4.4.5 Document control 4.5.3 Records
5. Product risk characterization: Characterizes new and existing products with respect to their risk using information about health, safety, and environmental hazards and reasonably foreseeable exposures. Establishes a system that initiates re-evaluation.	4.3.1 Environmental aspects
6. Risk-management system: Establishes a system to identify, document, and implement health, safety and environmental risk-management actions appropriate to the product risks.	4.4.6 Operational control
7. Product and process design and improvement: Establishes and maintains a system that makes health, safety and environmental impacts including the use of energy and natural resources key considerations in designing, developing and improving products and processes.	4.3.1 Environmental aspects 4.3.3 Objectives and targets

8. Employee education and product use feedback: Educates and trains employees, based on job function, on the proper handling, recycling, use, and disposal of products and known product uses. Implements a system that encourages employees to feed back information on new uses, identified misuses or adverse effects for use in product risk characterization.	4.4.2 Training, awareness and competence
9. Contract manufacturers: Selects contract manufacturers who employ appropriate practices for health, safety and environmental protection for the operations under contract, or works with contract manufacturers to help them implement such practices. Provides information and guidance appropriate to the product and process risk to foster proper handling, use, recycling and disposal. Periodically reviews performance of contract manufacturers.	N/A
10. Suppliers: Requires suppliers to provide appropriate health, safety and environmental information and guidance on their products. Factors adherence to sound health, safety, and environmental principles, such as those contained in Responsible Care® into procurement decisions.	N/A
11. Distributors: Provides health, safety and environmental information to distributors. Commensurate with product risks, selects, works with and periodically reviews distributors to foster proper use, handling, recycling, disposal and transmittal of appropriate information to downstream users. When a company identifies improper practices involving a products, it will work with the distributor to improve those practices. If, in the company's independent	4.4.3 Communication

judgement, improvement is not evident, then the company should take further measures—up to and including termination of the business relationship. This management Practice should be implemented in conjunction with the Distribution Code of Management Practices.

12. Customers and other direct product receivers: Provides health, safety and environmental information to direct product receivers. Commensurate with product risk, works with them to foster proper use, handling, recycling, disposal and transmittal of appropriate information to downstream users. When a company identifies improper practices involving a product, it will work with the product receiver to improve those practices. If, in the company's independent judgement, improvement is not evident, then the company should take further measures up to and including termination of product sale.

4.4.3 Communication

Distribution

Risk Management

1.1 Regular evaluations of chemical distribution risks which consider the hazards of the material, the likelihood of accidents/incidents and the potential for human and environmental exposure from release of the material over the route of transport.

4.4.7 Emergency preparedness and response

1.2 Implementation of chemical distribution risk reduction measures that are appropriate to the risk level.

4.4.6 Operational control

1.3 Internal reporting and investigation of chemical distribution accidents/incidents, and implementation of preventive measures.

4.5.1 Monitoring and measurement

4.5.2 Nonconformance and corrective and preventive action

Compliance Review and Training	
2.1 A process for monitoring changes and interpretations of new and existing regulations and industry standards for their applicability to the company's chemical distribution activities, and for implementing those regulations and standards.	4.3.2 Legal and other requirements
2.2 Training for all affected company employees in the proper implementation of applicable regulations and company requirements.	4.4.2 Training, awareness and competence
2.3 A program for providing guidance and information to carriers, distributors and contractors who perform distribution activities for the company on the company's training and compliance requirements for the activities.	4.4.3 Communication
2.4 Regular reviews of company employee, carrier, distributor and contractor compliance with applicable regulations and company requirements.	4.4.2 Training, awareness and competence
Carrier Safety	
3.1 A process for qualifying carriers of all modes and types (common, contract, private and customer controlled) that transport chemicals to and from company facilities that emphasizes carrier safety fitness and regulatory compliance, and includes regular reviews of their performance and compliance.	4.3.1 Environmental aspects
3.2 Feedback to carriers on their safety performance and suggestions for improvement.	4.4.3 Communication
Handling and Storage	
4.1 Documented procedures for the selection and use of containers that are appropriate for the chemical being shipped, in compliance with testing and certification requirements, and free of leaks and visible defects.	4.4.6 Operational control

4.4.6 Operational control

4.4.6 Operational control

4.4.6 Operational control

4.4.3 Communication

N/A

N/A

4.4.7 Emergency preparedness and response

4.2 Documented procedures for loading chemicals at company facilities that will reduce emissions to the environment, protect personnel and provide securement of the lading during transit.

4.4.7 Emergency preparedness and response

N/A

4.3 Documented procedures for unloading chemicals at company facilities that will reduce emissions to the environment, protect personnel and provide for safe unloading into proper storage facilities.

4.4.7 Emergency preparedness and response

4.4 Defined criteria for the cleaning and return of tank cars, tank trucks, marine vessels, and returnable/refillable bulk and semi-bulk containers, and for the proper disposal of cleaning residues.

4.4.3 Communication

4.5 A program for providing guidance and information to customers, distributors, and other receivers on proper procedures for unloading and storing the company's chemicals.

4.6 A process for selecting distributors and other facilities that store or handle the company's chemicals in transit that emphasizes safety fitness and regulatory compliance and includes regular reviews of their performance and compliance.

4.7 Feedback to distributors and operators of other facilities that store or handle chemicals in transit on their safety performance and suggestions for improvement.

Emergency Preparedness

5.1 A process for responding to chemical distribution accident/incidents involving the company's chemicals.

Appendix A

ISO 14001, *Environmental management systems—Specification with guidance for use*

INTRODUCTION

Organizations of all kinds are increasingly concerned to achieve and demonstrate sound environmental performance by controlling the impact of their activities, products or services on the environment, taking into account their environmental policy and objectives. They do so in the context of increasingly stringent legislation, the development of economic policies and other measures to foster environmental protection, and a general growth of concern from interested parties about environmental matters including sustainable development.

Many organizations have undertaken environmental "reviews" or "audits" to assess their environmental performance. On their own, however, these "reviews" and "audits" may not be sufficient to provide an organization with the assurance that its performance not only meets, but will continue to meet, its legal and policy requirements. To be effective, they need to be conducted within a structured management system and integrated with overall management activity.

International Standards covering environmental management are intended to provide organizations with the elements of an effective environmental management system which can be integrated with other management requirements, to assist organizations to achieve environmental and economic goals. These Standards, like other International Standards, are not intended to be used to create non-tariff trade barriers or to increase or change an organization's legal obligations.

This International Standard specifies the requirements of such an environmental management system. It has been written to be applicable to all types and sizes of organizations and to accommodate diverse geographical, cultural and social conditions. The basis of the approach is shown in figure 1. [Note: Figure 1 is not included here.] The success of the system depends on commitment from all levels and functions, especially from top management. A ystem of this kind enables an organization to establish, and assess the effectiveness of, procedures to set an environmental policy and objectives, achieve conformance with them, and demonstrate such conformance to others. The overall aim of this International Standard is to support environmental protection and prevention of pollution in balance with socio-economic needs. It should be noted that many of the requirements may be addressed concurrently or revisited at any time.

There is an important distinction between this specification which describes the requirements for certification/registration and/or self-declaration of an organization's environmental management system and a non-certifiable guideline intended to provide generic assistance to an organization for implementing or improving an environmental management system. Environmental management encompasses a full range of issues including those with strategic and competitive implications. Demonstration of successful implementation of this International Standard can be used by an organization to assure interested parties that an appropriate environmental management system is in place.

Guidance on supporting environmental management techniques will be contained in other International Standards.

This International Standard contains only those requirements that may be objectively audited for certification/registration purposes and/or self-declaration purposes. Those organizations requiring more general guidance on a broad range of environmental management system issues should refer to ISO 14004:1996, *Environmental management systems—*

General guidelines on principles, systems and supporting techniques.

It should be noted that this International Standard does not establish absolute requirements for environmental performance beyond commitment, in the policy, to compliance with applicable legislation and regulations and to continual improvement. Thus, two organizations carrying out similar activities but having different environmental performance may both comply with its requirements.

The adoption and implementation of a range of environmental management techniques in a systematic manner can contribute to optimal outcomes for all interested parties. However, adoption of this International Standard will not in itself guarantee optimal environmental outcomes. In order to achieve environmental objectives, the environmental management system should encourage organizations to consider implementation of the best available technology, where appropriate and where economically viable. In addition, the cost effectiveness of such technology should be fully taken into account.

This International Standard is not intended to address, and does not include requirements for, aspects of occupational health and safety management; however, it does not seek to discourage an organization from developing integration of such management system elements. Nevertheless, the certification/registration process will only be applicable to aspects of the environmental management system.

This International Standard shares common management system principles with the ISO 9000 series of quality system Standards. Organizations may elect to use an existing management system consistent with the ISO 9000 series as a basis for its environmental management system. It should be understood, however, that the application of various elements of the management system may differ due to different purposes and different interested parties. While quality management systems deal with customer needs, environmental management systems address the needs of a broad range of interested parties and the evolving needs of society for environmental protection.

The environmental management system requirements specified in this International Standard do not need to be established independently of existing management system elements. In some cases, it will be possible to comply with the requirements by adapting existing management system elements.

1 SCOPE

This International Standard specifies requirements for an environmental management system, to enable an organization to formulate a policy and objectives taking into account legislative requirements and information about significant environmental impacts. It applies to those environmental aspects which the organization can control and over which it can be expected to have an influence. It does not itself state specific environmental performance criteria.

This International Standard is applicable to any organization that wishes to

a) implement, maintain and improve an environmental management system;

b) assure itself of its conformance with its stated environmental policy;

c) demonstrate such conformance to others;

d) seek certification/registration of its environmental management system by an external organization;

e) make a self-determination and declaration of conformance with this International Standard.

All the requirements in this International Standard are intended to be incorporated into any environmental management system. The extent of the application will depend on such factors as the environmental policy of the organization, the nature of its activities and the conditions in which it operates. This International Standard also provides, in annex A, informative guidance on the use of the specification.

The scope of any application of this International Standard must be clearly identified.

NOTE—For ease of use, the subclause of the specification and annex A have related numbers; thus, for example, 4.3.3 and A.3.3 both deal with environmental objectives and targets, and 4.5.4 and A.5.4 both deal with environmental management system audit.

2 NORMATIVE REFERENCES

There are no normative references at present.

3 DEFINITIONS

For the purposes of this International Standard, the following definitions apply.

3.1 continual improvement

process of enhancing the environmental management system to achieve improvements in overall environmental performance in line with the organization's environmental policy

NOTE—The process need not take place in all areas of activity simultaneously.

3.2 environment

surroundings in which an organization operates, including air, water, land, natural resources, flora, fauna, humans, and their interrelation

NOTE—Surroundings in this context extend from within an organization to the global system.

3.3 environmental aspect

element of an organization's activities, products or services that can interact with the environment

NOTE—A significant environmental aspect is an environmental aspect that has or can have a significant environmental impact.

3.4 environmental impact

any change to the environment, whether adverse or beneficial, wholly or partially resulting from an organization's activities, products or services

3.5 environmental management system

the part of the overall management system that includes organizational structure, planning activities, responsibilities, practices, procedures, processes and resources for developing, implementing, achieving, reviewing and maintaining the environmental policy

3.6 environmental management system audit

a systematic and documented verification process of objectively obtaining and evaluating evidence to determine whether an organization's environmental management system conforms to the environmental management system audit criteria set by the organization, and for communication of the results of this process to management

3.7 environmental objective

overall environmental goal, arising from the environmental policy, that an organization sets itself to achieve, and which is quantified where practicable

3.8 environmental performance

measurable results of the environmental management system, related to an organization's control of its environmental aspects, based on its environmental policy, objectives and targets

3.9 environmental policy

statement by the organization of its intentions and principles in relation to its overall environmental performance which provides a framework for action and for the setting of its environmental objectives and targets

3.10 environmental target

detailed performance requirement, quantified where practicable, applicable to the organization or parts thereof, that arises from the environmental objectives and that needs to be set and met in order to achieve those objectives

3.11 interested party
individual or group concerned with or affected by the environmental performance of an organization

3.12 organization
company, corporation, firm, enterprise, authority or institution, or part or combination thereof, whether incorporated or not, public or private, that has its own functions and administration

NOTE—For organizations with more than one operating unit, a single operating unit may be defined as an organization.

3.13 prevention of pollution
use of processes, practices, materials or products that avoid, reduce or control pollution, which may include recycling, treatment, process changes, control mechanisms, efficient use of resources and material substitution

NOTE—The potential benefits of prevention of pollution include the reduction of adverse environmental impacts, improved efficiency and reduced costs.

4 ENVIRONMENTAL MANAGEMENT SYSTEM REQUIREMENTS

4.1 General
The organization shall establish and maintain an environmental management system, the requirements of which are described in the whole of clause 4.

4.2 Environmental policy
Top management shall define the organization's environmental policy and ensure that it

a) is appropriate to the nature, scale and environmental impacts of its activities, products or services;

b) includes a commitment to continual improvement and prevention of pollution;

c) includes a commitment to comply with relevant environmental legislation and regulations, and with other requirements to which the organization subscribes;

d) provides the framework for setting and reviewing environmental objectives and targets;

e) is documented, implemented and maintained and communicated to all employees;

f) is available to the public.

4.3 Planning

4.3.1 Environmental aspects
The organization shall establish and maintain (a) procedure(s) to identify the environmental aspects of its activities, products or services that it can control and over which it can be expected to have an influence, in order to determine those which have or can have significant impacts on the environment. The organization shall ensure that the aspects related to these significant impacts are considered in setting its environmental objectives.

The organization shall keep this information up-to-date.

4.3.2 Legal and other requirements

The organization shall establish and maintain a procedure to identify and have access to legal and other requirements to which the organization subscribes, that are applicable to the environmental aspects of its activities, products or services.

4.3.3 Objectives and targets

The organization shall establish and maintain documented environmental objectives and targets, at each relevant function and level within the organization.

When establishing and reviewing its objectives, an organization shall consider the legal and other requirements, its significant environmental aspects, its technological options, and its financial, operational and business requirements, and the views of interested parties.

The objectives and targets shall be consistent with the environmental policy, including the commitment to prevention of pollution.

4.3.4 Environmental management programme(s)

The organization shall establish and maintain (a) program(s) for achieving its objectives and targets. It shall include:

a) designation of responsibility for achieving objectives and targets at each relevant function and level of the organization;

b) the means and time-frame by which they are to be achieved.

If a project relates to new developments and new or modified activities, products or services, programme(s) shall be amended where relevant to ensure that environmental management applies to such projects.

4.4 Implementation and operation

4.4.1 Structure and responsibility

Roles, responsibility and authorities shall be defined, documented and communicated in order to facilitate effective environmental management.

Management shall provide resources essential to the implementation and control of the environmental management system. Resources include human resources and specialized skills, technology and financial resources.

The organization's top management shall appoint (a) specific management representative(s) who, irrespective of other responsibilities, shall have defined roles, responsibilities and authority for

a) ensuring that environmental management system requirements are established, implemented and maintained in accordance with this International Standard;

b) reporting on the performance of the environmental management system to top management for review and as a basis for improvement of the environmental management system.

4.4.2 Training, awareness and competence

The organization shall identify training needs. It shall require that all personnel whose work may create a significant impact upon the environment, have received appropriate training.

It shall establish and maintain procedures to make its employees or members at each relevant function and level aware of

a) the importance of conformance with the environmental policy and procedures and with the requirements of the environmental management system;

b) the significant environmental impacts, actual or potential, of their work activities and the environmental benefits of improved personal performance;

c) their roles and responsibilities in achieving conformance with the environmental policy and procedures and with the requirements of the environmental management system, including emergency preparedness and response requirements;

d) the potential consequences of departure from specified operating procedures.

Personnel performing the tasks which can cause significant environmental impacts shall be competent on the basis of appropriate education, training and/or experience.

4.4.3 Communication
With regard to its environmental aspects and environmental management system, the organization shall establish and maintain procedures for

a) internal communication between the various levels and functions of the organization;

b) receiving, documenting and responding to relevant communication from external interested parties.

The organization shall consider processes for external communication on its significant environmental aspects and record its decision.

4.4.4 Environmental management system documentation
The organization shall establish and maintain information, in paper or electronic form, to

a) describe the core elements of the management system and their interaction;

b) provide direction to related documentation.

4.4.5 Document control
The organization shall establish and maintain procedures for controlling all documents required by this International Standard to ensure that

a) they can be located;

b) they are periodically reviewed, revised as necessary, and approved for adequacy by authorized personnel;

c) the current versions of relevant documents are available at all locations where operations essential to the effective functioning of the environmental management system are performed;

d) obsolete documents are promptly removed from all points of issue and points of use or otherwise assured against unintended use;

e) any obsolete documents retained for legal and/or knowledge preservation purposes are suitably identified.

Documentation shall be legible, dated (with dates of revision), and readily identifiable, maintained in an orderly manner and retained for a specified period. Procedures and responsibilities shall be established and maintained concerning the creation and modification of the various types of document.

4.4.6 Operational control

The organization shall identify those operations and activities that are associated with the identified significant environmental aspects in line with its policy, objectives and targets. The organization shall plan these activities, including maintenance, in order to ensure that they are carried out under specified conditions by

a) establishing and maintaining documented procedures to cover situations where their absence could lead to deviations from the environmental policy and the objectives and targets;

b) stipulating operating criteria in the procedures;

c) establishing and maintaining procedures related to the identifiable significant environmental aspects of goods and services used by the organization and communicating relevant procedures and requirements to suppliers and contractors.

4.4.7 Emergency preparedness and response

The organization shall establish and maintain procedures to identify potential for and respond to accidents and emergency situations, and for preventing and mitigating the environmental impacts that may be associated with them.

The organization shall review and revise, where necessary, its emergency preparedness and response procedures, in particular, after the occurrence of accidents or emergency situations.

The organization shall also periodically test such procedures where practicable.

4.5 Checking and corrective action

4.5.1 Monitoring and measurement

The organization shall establish and maintain documented procedures to monitor and measure, on a regular basis, the key characteristics of its operations and activities that can have a significant impact on the environment. This shall include the recording of information to track performance, relevant operational controls, and conformance with the organization's environmental objectives and targets.

Monitoring equipment shall be calibrated and maintained and records of this process shall be retained according to the organization's procedures.

The organization shall establish and maintain a documented procedure for periodically evaluating compliance with relevant environmental legislation and regulations.

4.5.2 Nonconformance and corrective and preventive action

The organization shall establish and maintain procedures for defining responsibility and authority for handling and investigating nonconformance, taking action to mitigate any impacts caused and for initiating and completing corrective and preventive action.

Any corrective or preventive action taken to eliminate the causes of actual and potential nonconformances shall be appropriate to the magnitude of problems and commensurate with the environmental impact encountered.

The organization shall implement and record any changes in the documented procedures resulting from corrective and preventive action.

4.5.3 Records

The organization shall establish and maintain procedures for the identification, maintenance and disposition of environmental records. These records shall include training records and the results of audits and reviews.

Environmental records shall be legible, identifiable and traceable to the activity, product or service involved. Environmental records shall be stored and maintained in such a way that they are readily retrievable and protected against damage, deterioration or loss. Their retention times shall be established and recorded.

Records shall be maintained, as appropriate to the system and to the organization, to demonstrate conformance to the requirements of this International Standard.

4.5.4 Environmental management system audit

The organization shall establish and maintain (a) programme(s) and procedures for periodic environmental management system audits to be carried out, in order to

a) determine whether or not the environmental management system

   1) conforms to planned arrangements for environmental management, including the requirements of this International Standard; and

   2) has been properly implemented and maintained; and

b) provide information on the results of audits to management.

The organization's audit programme, including any schedule, shall be based on the environmental importance of the activity concerned and the results of previous audits. In order to be comprehensive, the audit procedures shall cover the audit scope, frequency and methodologies, as well as the responsibilities and requirements for conducting audits and reporting results.

4.6 Management review

The organization's top management shall, at intervals that it determines, review the environmental management system, to ensure its continuing suitability, adequacy and effectiveness. The management review process shall ensure that the necessary information is collected to allow management to carry out this evaluation. This review shall be documented.

The management review shall address the possible need for changes to policy, objectives and other elements of the environmental management system, in the light of environmental management system audit results, changing circumstances and the commitment to continual improvement.

ANNEX A (INFORMATIVE)

GUIDANCE ON THE USE OF THE SPECIFICATION

This annex gives additional information on the requirements and is intended to avoid misinterpretation of the specification. This annex only addresses the requirements contained in environmental management system clause 4.

A.1 General requirements

It is intended that the implementation of an environmental management system described by the specification will result in improved environmental performance. The specification is based on the concept that the organization will periodically review and evaluate its environmental management system in order to identify opportunities for improvement and their implementation. Improvements in its environmental management system are intended to result in additional improvements in environmental performance.

The environmental management system provides a structured process for the achievement of continual improvement, the rate and extent of which will be determined by the organization in the light of economic and other circumstances. Although some improvement in environmental performance can be expected due to the adoption of a systematic approach, it should be understood that the environmental management system is a tool which enables the organization to achieve and systematically control the level of environmental performance that it sets itself. The establishment and operation of an environmental management system will not, in itself, necessarily result in an immediate reduction of adverse environmental impact.

An organization has the freedom and flexibility to define its boundaries and may choose to implement this International Standard with respect to the entire organization, or to specific operating units or activities of the organization. If this International Standard is implemented for a specific operating unit or activity, policies and procedures developed by other parts of the organization can be used to meet the requirements of this International Standard, provided that they are applicable to the specific operating unit or activity that will be subject to it. The level of detail and complexity of the environmental management system, the extent of documentation and the resources devoted to it will be dependent on the size of an organization and the nature of its activities. This may be the case in particular for small and medium-sized enterprises.

Integration of environmental matters with the overall management system can contribute to the effective implementation of the environmental management system, as well as to efficiency and to clarity of roles.

This International Standard contains management system requirements, based on the dynamic cyclical process of "plan, implement, check and review".

The system should enable an organization to

a) establish an environmental policy appropriate to itself;

b) identify the environmental aspects arising from the organization's past, existing or planned activities, products or services, to determine the environmental impacts of significance;

c) identify the relevant legislative and regulatory requirements;

d) identify priorities and set appropriate environmental objectives and targets;

e) establish a structure and (a) programme(s) to implement the policy and achieve objectives and targets;

f) facilitate planning, control, monitoring, corrective action, auditing and review activities to ensure both that the policy is complied with and that the environmental management system remains appropriate;

g) be capable of adapting to changing circumstances.

A.2 Environmental policy

The environmental policy is the driver for implementing and improving the organization's environmental management system so that it can maintain and potentially improve its environmental performance. The policy should therefore reflect the commitment of top management to compliance with applicable laws and continual improvement. The policy forms the basis upon which the organization sets its objectives and targets. The policy should be sufficiently clear to be capable of being understood by internal and external interested parties and should be periodically reviewed and revised to reflect changing conditions and information. Its area of application should be clearly identifiable.

The organization's top management should define and document its environmental policy within the context of the environmental policy of any broader corporate body of which it is a part and with the endorsement of that body, if there is one.

NOTE—Top management may consist of an individual or group of individuals with executive responsibility for the organization.

A.3 Planning

A.3.1 Environmental aspects

Subclause 4.3.1 is intended to provide a process for an organization to identify significant environmental aspects that should be addressed as a priority by the organization's environmental management system. This process should take into account the cost and time of undertaking the analysis and the availability of reliable data. Information already developed for regulatory or other purposes may be used in this process. Organizations may also take into account the degree of practical control they may have over the environmental aspects being considered. Organizations should determine what their environmental aspect are, taking into account the inputs and outputs associated with their current and relevant past activities, products and/or services.

An organization with no existing environmental management system should, initially, establish its current position with regard to the environment by means of a review. The aim should be to consider all environmental aspects of the organization as a basis for establishing the environmental management system.

Those organizations with operating environmental management systems do not have to undertake such a review.

The review should cover four key areas:

a) legislative and regulatory requirements;

b) an identification of significant environmental aspects;

c) an examination of all existing environmental management practices and procedures;

d) an evaluation of feedback from the investigation of previous incidents.

In all cases, consideration should be given to normal and abnormal operations within the organization, and to potential emergency conditions.

A suitable approach to the review may include checklists, interviews, direct inspection and measurement, results of previous audits or other reviews depending on the nature of the activities.

The process to identify the significant environmental aspects associated with the activities at operating units should, where relevant, consider

a) emissions to air;

b) releases to water;

c) waste management;

d) contamination of land;

e) use of raw materials and natural resources;

f) other local environmental and community issues.

This process should consider normal operating conditions, shut-down and start-up conditions, as well as the realistic potential significant impacts associated with reasonably foreseeable or emergency situations.

The process is intended to identify significant environmental aspects associated with activities, products or services, and is not intended to require a detailed life cycle assessment. Organizations do not have to evaluate each product, component or raw material input. They may select categories of activities, products or services to identify those aspects most likely to have a significant impact.

The control and influence over the environmental aspects of products vary significantly, depending on the market situation of the organization. A contractor or supplier to the organization may have comparatively little control, while the organization responsible for product design can alter the aspects significantly by changing, for example, a single input material. Whilst recognizing that organizations may have limited control over the use and disposal of their products, they should consider, where practical, proper handling and disposal mechanisms. This provision is not intended to change or increase an organization's legal obligations.

A.3.2 Legal and other requirements

Examples of other requirements to which the organization may subscribe are

a) industry codes of practice;

b) agreements with public authorities;

c) non-regulatory guidelines.

A.3.3 Objectives and targets

The objectives should be specific and targets should be measurable wherever practicable, and where appropriate take preventative measures into account.

When considering their technological options, an organization may consider the use of the best available technology where economically viable, cost-effective and judged appropriate.

The reference to the financial requirements of the organization is not intended to imply that organizations are obliged to use environmental cost-accounting methodologies.

A.3.4 Environmental management programme(s)

The creation and use of one or more programmes is a key element to the successful implementation of an environmental management system. The programme should describe how the organization's objectives and targets will be achieved, including time-scales and personnel responsible for implementing the organization's environmental policy. This programme may be subdivided to address specific elements of the organization's operations. The programme should include an environmental review for new activities.

The programme may include, where appropriate and practical, consideration of planning, design, production, marketing and disposal stages. This may be undertaken for both current and new activities, products or services. For products this may address design, materials, production processes, use and ultimate disposal. For installations or significant modifications of processes this may address planning, design, construction, commissioning, operation and, at the appropriate time determined by the organization, decommissioning.

A.4 Implementation and operation

A.4.1 Structure and responsibility

The successful implementation of an environmental management system calls for the commitment of all employees of the organization. Environmental responsibilities therefore should not be seen as confined to the environmental function, but may also include other areas of an organization, such as operational management or staff functions other than environmental.

This commitment should begin at the highest levels of management. Accordingly, top management should establish the organization's environmental policy and ensure that the environmental management system is implemented. As part of this commitment, the top management should designate (a) specific management representative(s) with defined responsibility and authority for implementing the environmental management system. In large or complex organizations there may be more than one designated representative. In small or medium sized enterprises, these responsibilities may be undertaken by one individual. Top management should also ensure that appropriate resources are provided to ensure that the environmental management system is implemented and maintained. It is also important that the key environmental management system responsibilities are well defined and communicated to the relevant personnel.

A.4.2 Training, awareness and competence

The organization should establish and maintain procedures for identifying training needs. The organization should also require that contractors working on its behalf are able to demonstrate that their employees have the requisite training.

Management should determine the level of experience, competence and training necessary to ensure the capability of personnel, especially those carrying out specialized environmental management functions.

A.4.3 Communication

Organizations should implement a procedure for receiving, documenting and responding to relevant information and requests from interested parties. This procedure may include a dialogue with interested parties and consideration of their relevant concerns. In some circumstances, responses to interested parties' concerns may include relevant information about the environmental impacts associated with the organization's operations. These procedures should also address necessary communications with public authorities regarding emergency planning and other relevant issues.

A.4.4 Environmental management system documentation

The level of detail of the documentation should be sufficient to describe the core elements of the environmental management system and their interaction and provide direction on where to obtain more detailed information on the operation of specific parts of the environmental management system. This documentation may be integrated with documentation of other systems implemented by the organization. It does not have to be in the form of a single manual.

Related documentation may include

a) process information;

b) organizational charts;

c) internal standards and operational procedures;

d) site emergency plans.

A.4.5 Document control
The intent of 4.4.5 is to ensure that organizations create and maintain documents in a manner sufficient to implement the environmental management system. However, the primary focus of organizations should be on the effective implementation of the environmental management system and on environmental performance and not on a complex documentation control system.

A.4.6 Operational control
Text may be included here in a future revision.

A.4.7 Emergency preparedness and response
Text may be included here in a future revision.

A.5 Checking and corrective action

A.5.1 Monitoring and measurement
Text may be included here in a future revision.

A.5.2 Nonconformance and corrective and preventive action
In establishing and maintaining procedures for investigating and correcting nonconformance, the organization should include these basic elements:

a) identifying the cause of the nonconformance;

b) identifying and implementing the necessary corrective action;

c) implementing or modifying controls necessary to avoid repetition of the nonconformance;

d) recording any changes in written procedures resulting from the corrective action.

Depending on the situation, this may be accomplished rapidly and with a minimum of formal planning or it may be a more complex and long-term activity. The associated documentation should be appropriate to the level of corrective action.

A.5.3 Records
Procedures for identification, maintenance and disposition of records should focus on those records needed for the implementation and operation of the environmental management system and for recording the extent to which planned objectives and targets have been met.

Environmental records may include

a) information on applicable environmental laws or other requirements;

b) complaint records;

c) training records;

d) process information;

e) product information;

f) inspection, maintenance and calibration records;

g) pertinent contractor and supplier information;

h) incident reports;

i) information on emergency preparedness and response;

j) records of significant environmental aspects;

k) audit results;

l) management reviews.

Proper account should be taken of confidential business information.

A.5.4 Environmental management system audit

The audit program and procedures should cover

a) the activities and areas to be considered in audits;

b) the frequency of audits;

c) the responsibilities associated with managing and conducting audits;

d) the communication of audit results;

e) auditor competence;

f) how audits will be conducted.

Audits may be performed by personnel from within the organization and/or by external persons selected by the organization. In either case the persons conducting the audit should be in a position to do so impartially and objectively.

A.6 Management review

In order to maintain continual improvement, suitability and effectiveness of the environmental management system, and thereby its performance, the organization's management should review and evaluate the environmental management system at defined intervals. The scope of the review should be comprehensive, though not all elements of an environmental management system need to be reviewed at once and the review process may take place over a period of time.

The review of the policy, objectives and procedures should be carried out by the level of management that defined them.

Reviews should include

a) results from audits;

b) the extent to which objectives and targets have been met;

c) the continuing suitability of the environmental management system in relation to changing conditions and information;

d) concerns among relevant interested parties.

Observations, conclusions and recommendations should be documented for necessary action.

ANNEX B (INFORMATIVE)

LINKS BETWEEN ISO 14001 AND ISO 9001

Tables B.1 and B.2 identify links and broad technical correspondences between ISO 14001 and ISO 9001 and *vice versa.*

The objective of the comparison is to demonstrate the combinability of both systems to those organizations already operating one of these International Standards and which may wish to operate both.

A direct link between subclauses of the two International Standards has only been established if the two subclauses are largely congruent in requirements. Beyond that, many detailed cross-connections of minor relevance exist which could not be shown here.

ANNEX C (INFORMATIVE)

BIBLIOGRAPHY

[1] ISO 9001-1:1994, *Quality management and quality assurance standards—Part 1: Guidelines for selection and use.*

[2] ISO 9000-2:1993, *Quality management and quality assurance standards—Part 2: Generic guidelines for the application of ISO 9001, ISO 9002 and ISO 9003.*

[3] ISO 9000-3:1991, *Quality management and quality assurance standards—Part 3: Guidelines for the application of ISO 9001 to the development, supply and maintenance of software.*

[4] ISO 9000-4:1993, *Quality management and quality assurance standards—Part 4: Guide to dependability programme management.*

[5] ISO 9001:1994, *Quality systems—Model for quality assurance in design, development, production, installation and servicing.*

[6] ISO 14004:1996, *Environmental management systems—General guidelines on principles, systems and supporting techniques.*

[7] ISO 14010:1996, *Guidelines for environmental auditing—General principles.*

[8] ISO 14011:1996, *Guidelines for environmental auditing—Audit procedures—Auditing of environmental management systems.*

[9] ISO 14012:1996, *Guidelines for environmental auditing—Qualification criteria for environmental auditors.*

Table B.1. Correspondence between ISO 14001 and ISO 9001.

ISO 14001:1996		ISO 9001:1994	
General requirements	4.1	4.2.1 1st sentence	General
Environmental policy	4.2	4.1.1	Quality policy
Planning			
Environmental aspects	4.3.1	— [1)]	—
Legal and other requirements	4.3.2	— [2)]	—
Objectives and targets	4.3.3	—	—
Environmental management programme(s)	4.3.4	4.2.3	Quality planning
	—		
Implementation and operation			
Structure and responsibility	4.4.1	4.1.2	Organization
Training, awareness and competence	4.4.2	4.18	Training
Communication	4.4.3	—	
Environmental management system documentation	4.4.4	4.2.1 without 1st sentence	General
Document control	4.4.5	4.5	Document and data control
Operational control	4.4.6	4.2.2	Quality system procedures
	4.4.6	4.3 [3)]	Contract review
	4.4.6	4.4	Design control
	4.4.6	4.6	Purchasing
	4.4.6	4.7	Control of customer-supplied product
	4.4.6	4.9	Process control
	4.4.6	4.15	Handling, storage, packaging, preservation and delivery

Table B.1. (*continued*).

ISO 14001:1996			ISO 9001:1994
Operational control	4.4.6	4.19	Servicing
		4.8	Product identification and traceability
Emergency preparedness and response	4.4.7	—	—
Checking and corrective action			
Monitoring and measurement	4.5.1 1st and 3rd paragraphs	4.10	Inspection and testing
	—	4.12	Inspection and test status
	—	4.20	Statistical techniques
Monitoring and measurement	4.5.1 2nd paragraph	4.11	Control of inspection, measuring and test equipment
Nonconformance and corrective and preventive action	4.5.2 1st part of 1st sentence	4.13	Control of nonconforming product
Nonconformance and corrective and preventive action	4.5.2 without 1st part of 1st sentence	4.14	Corrective and preventive action
Records	4.5.3	4.16	Control of quality records
Environmental management system audit	4.5.4	4.17	Internal quality audits
Management review	4.6	4.1.3	Management review

1) Legal requirements addressed in ISO 9001, 4.4.4.
2) Objectives addressed in ISO 9001, 4.1.1.
3) Communication with the quality stakeholders (customers).

Table B.2. Correspondence between ISO 9001 and ISO 14001.

ISO 9001:1994			ISO 14001:1996
Management responsibility			
Quality policy	4.1.1	4.2	Environmental policy
	—[1]	4.3.1	Environmental aspects
	—[2]	4.3.2	Legal and other requirements
	—	4.3.3	Objectives and targets
	—	4.3.4	Environmental management programmes(s)
Organization	4.1.2	4.4.1	Structure and responsibility
Management review	4.1.3	4.6	Management review
Quality system			
General	4.2.1 1st sentence	4.1	General requirements
	4.2.1 without 1st sentence	4.4.4	Environmental management system documentation
Quality system procedures	4.2.2	4.4.6	Operational control
Quality planning	4.2.3	—	
Contract review	4.3[3]	4.4.6	Operational control
Design control	4.4	4.4.6	Operational control
Document and data control	4.5	4.4.5	Document control
Purchasing	4.6	4.4.6	Operational control
Control of customer-supplied product	4.7	4.4.6	Operational control

Table B.2. (*continued*).

ISO 9001:1994			ISO 14001
Product identification and traceability	4.8	—	—
Process control	4.9	4.6	Operational control
Inspection and testing	4.10	4.5.1 1st and 3rd paragraph	Monitoring and measurement
Control of inspection, measuring and test equipment	4.11	4.5.1 2nd paragraph	Monitoring and measurement
Inspection and test status	4.12	—	—
Control of nonconforming product	4.13	4.5.2 1st part of 1st sentence	Nonconformance and corrective and preventive action
Corrective and preventive action	4.14	4.5.2 1st without 1st part of 1st sentence	Nonconformance and corrective and preventive action
	—	4.4.7	Emergency preparedness and response
Handling, storage, packaging, preservation and delivery	4.15	4.4.6	Operational control
Control of quality records	4.16	4.5.3	Records
Internal quality audits	4.17	4.5.4	Environmental management system audit
Training	4.18	4.4.2	Training, awareness and competence
Servicing	4.19	4.4.6	Operational control
Statistical techniques	4.20	—	
	—	4.4.3	Communication

1) Legal requirements addressed in ISO 9001, 4.4.4.
2) Objectives addressed in ISO 9001, 4.1.1.
3) Communication with the quality stakeholders (customers).

Appendix B

Tables of Contents for ISO 14000 Series Standards

ISO 14001, Environmental management systems—Specification with guidance for use

Introduction

1 Scope

2 References

3 Definitions

4 Environmental management system

  4.1 General

  4.2 Environmental policy

  4.3 Planning
    4.3.1 Environmental aspects
    4.3.2 Legal and other requirements
    4.3.3 Objectives and targets
    4.3.4 Environmental management programme(s)

  4.4 Implementation and operation
    4.4.1 Structure and responsibility
    4.4.2 Training, awareness and competence
    4.4.3 Communication
    4.4.4 Environmental management system documentation
    4.4.5 Document control
    4.4.6 Operational control
    4.4.7 Emergency preparedness and response

  4.5 Checking and corrective action
    4.5.1 Monitoring and measurement
    4.5.2 Nonconformance and corrective and preventive action

ISO 14004, Environmental management systems— General guidelines on principles, systems and supporting techniques

ISO 14010, Guidelines for environmental auditing— General principles

5 General principles

   5.1 Objectives and scope

   5.2 Objectivity, independence and competence

   5.3 Due professional care

   5.4 Systematic procedures

   5.5 Audit criteria, evidence and findings

   5.6 Reliability of audit findings and conclusions

   5.7 Reporting

ISO 14011, Guidelines for environmental auditing— Auditing of environmental management systems

1 Scope

2 Normative references

3 Definitions

4 Environmental management system audit objectives, roles and responsibilities

   4.1 Audit objectives

   4.2 Roles, responsibilities and activities

      4.2.1 Lead auditor

      4.2.2 Auditor

      4.2.3 Audit team

      4.2.4 Client

      4.2.5 Auditee

5 Auditing

   5.1 Initiating the audit

      5.1.1 Audit scope

      5.1.2 Preliminary document review

   5.2 Preparing the audit

      5.2.1 Audit plan

      5.2.2 Audit team assignments

      5.2.3 Working documents

ISO 14012, Guidelines for environmental auditing— Qualification criteria for environmental auditors

Annex B   Environmental auditor registration body
B.1 General
B.2 Auditor registration

ISO 14020, General principles for all environmental labels and declarations

0   Introduction

1   Scope

2   Objective

3   Normative references

4   Definitions

5   General principles

ISO 14021, Environmental labels and declarations— Self-declaration environmental claims— Terms and definitions

0   Introduction

1   Scope

2   Objective

3   Definitions

4   Requirements

    4.1   General requirements

    4.2   Use of a symbol

    4.3   Specific requirements

    4.4   Verification requirements

5   Vague or non-specific environmental claims

6   Selected terms

    6.1   General

    6.2   Manufacturing and distribution
        6.2.1   Recycled content/material
        6.2.2   Reduced resource use

ISO 14022, *Environmental labels and declarations—Self-declaration environmental claims—Symbols*

ISO 14024, Environmental labeling—Type I guiding principles and procedures

0   Introduction

1   Scope

2   Objectives

3   Normative references

4   Definitions

5   Guiding principles and practices

    5.1   Voluntary nature of the program

    5.2   Relationship with regulations

    5.3   Life cycle consideration

    5.4   Selectivity

    5.5   Product environmental criteria
        5.5.1   Life cycle considerations
        5.5.2   Basis of criteria
        5.5.3   Period of validity
        5.5.4   Review period

    5.6   Product function characteristics

    5.7   Consultation

    5.8   Transparency

    5.9   International trade aspects

    5.10 Compliance

    5.11 Accessibility

    5.12 Objectivity, impartiality and scientific basis of product environmental criteria

    5.13 Avoidance of conflict of interest

    5.14 Costs and fees

    5.15 Confidentiality

6   Procedures for establishing program requirements

    6.1   Consultation with stakeholders

ISO 14031, Environmental performance evaluation guideline

0.1 Foreword

0.2 Introduction

1   Scope

2   Normative references

3   Definitions

4   Environmental performance evaluation (EPE)

    4.1   Planning EPE
        4.1.1   Management considerations
        4.1.2   Selecting indicators
            4.1.2.1 Selecting indicators for the management area
            4.1.2.2 Selecting indicators for the operational area
            4.1.2.3 Selecting indicators for the environmental area

    4.2   Evaluating environmental performance
        4.2.1   Collecting data
        4.2.2   Analyzing data
        4.2.3   Evaluating information
        4.2.4   Reporting and communicating
            4.2.4.1 Internal reporting and communicating
            4.2.4.2 External reporting and communicating

    4.3   Reviewing and improving EPE

Annex A Supplemental guidance on EPE

Annex B Bibliography

ISO 14040, Life cycle assessment—Principles and framework

0   Introduction

1   Scope

2   Definitions

3   General description of LCA

   3.1   Key features of LCA

   3.2   Phases of an LCA

4   Methodological framework

   4.1   Goal and scope definition
      4.1.1   Goal of the study
      4.1.2   Scope of the study
         4.1.2.1 Function and functional unit
         4.1.2.2 System boundaries
         4.1.2.3 Data quality requirements
         4.1.2.4 Comparisons between systems
         4.1.2.5 Critical review considerations

   4.2   Life cycle inventory analysis
      4.2.1   General description of life cycle inventory
      4.2.2   Data collection and calculation procedures

   4.3   Life cycle impact assessment

   4.4   Life cycle interpretation

5   Reporting

6   Critical review

   6.1   General description of critical reviews

   6.2   Need for critical review

   6.3   Critical review processes
      6.3.1   Internal review
      6.3.2   Expert review
      6.3.3   Review by interested parties

ISO 14041, Life cycle assessment—Inventory analysis

Foreword

0   Introduction

1   Scope

2   Normative references

3   Definitions

Annex A (informative) Example of a data collection sheet

Annex B (informative) Check-list of critical aspects of an LCA

Annex C (informative) Examples of different allocation procedures

ISO 14042, Life cycle assessment—Impact assessment

0 Foreword

1 Scope

2 Normative references

3 Definitions

4 Targets and purposes

5 Applications

    5.1 Fields of applications

    5.2 Internal vs. external use

6 Overview of life cycle impact assessment

    6.1 Classification

    6.2 Characterization

    6.3 Valuation

7 Planning life cycle impact assessment

8 Applying life cycle impact assessment

    8.1 LCIA as a comparative tool

        8.1.1 Methodological approach

        8.1.2 Procedure

        8.1.3 Data requirements

    8.2 LCIA as an explorative tool

        8.2.1 Methodological approach

        8.2.2 Procedure

        8.2.3 Data requirements

    8.3 LCIA as an indicative tool

        8.3.1 Methodological approach

        8.3.2 Procedure

        8.3.3 Data requirements

9 Reporting and critical review

9.1   Critical review

Annex I   Classification

Annex II   Characterization

Annex III Cause-effect chains

Annex IV Defining the basic LCA process

Annex V   Valuation

ISO 14060, Guide for the inclusion of environmental aspects in product standards

Introduction

1   Definitions

2   Purpose and scope

3   General considerations

4   How provisions in product standards can influence the environment

5   Environmental effects to be considered in product standards development

    5.1   General

    5.2   Inputs
        5.2.1   Material inputs
        5.2.2   Energy inputs

    5.3   Outputs
        5.3.1   Air emissions
        5.3.2   Water effluent
        5.3.3   Solid waste
        5.3.4   Other releases

6   Methodologies for identifying and assessing environmental effects

7   The relationship of product standards to environmental improvement strategies

    7.1   General

    7.2   Resource conservation

    7.3   Prevention of pollution

    7.4   Design for environment

Glossary

For the purposes of ISO 14001, the following definitions apply:

Continual improvement—Process of enhancing the environmental management system to achieve improvements in overall environmental performance in line with the organization's environmental policy. *Note:* The process need not take place in all areas of activity simultaneously.

Environment—Surroundings in which an organization operates, including air, water, land, natural resources, flora, fauna, humans, and their interrelation. *Note:* Surroundings in this context extend from within an organization to the global system.

Environmental aspect—Element of an organization's activities, products, or services that can interact with the environment.

Environmental impact—Any change to the environment, whether adverse or beneficial, wholly or partially resulting from an organization's activities, products, or services.

Environmental management system (EMS)—That part of the overall management system that includes organizational structure, planning activities, responsibilities, practices, procedures, processes, and resources for developing, implementing, achieving, reviewing, and maintaining the environmental policy.

Environmental management system audit—Systematic and documented verification process of objectively obtaining and evaluating evidence to determine whether an organization's environmental management system conforms to the environmental management system audit criteria set by the organization, and for communication of the results of this process to management. [Author's note: ISO 14011 uses the same definition, except that it specifies communication of the results of the process to *the client*.]

Environmental objective—Overall environmental goal, arising from the environmental policy, that an organization sets itself to achieve and that is quantified where practicable.

Environmental performance—Measurable results of the environmental management system, related to an organization's control of its environmental aspects, based on its environmental policy, objectives, and targets. [Author's note: ISO 14031 defines this term as *results of an organization's management of the environmental aspects of its activities, products, and services. Note: In the context of environmental management systems, results may be measured against the organization's policy, targets, and objectives.*]

Environmental policy—Statement by the organization of its intentions and principles in relation to its overall environmental performance, which provides a framework for action and for the setting of its environmental objectives and targets.

Environmental target—Detailed performance requirement, quantified where practicable, applicable to the organization or parts thereof, that arises from the environmental objectives and that needs to be set and met in order to achieve those objectives.

Interested party—Individual or group concerned with or affected by the environmental performance of an organization.

Organization—Company, corporation, firm, enterprise, authority, or institution, or part or combination thereof, whether incorporated or not, public or private, that has its own functions and administration. *Note:* For organizations with more than one operating unit, a single operating unit may be defined as an organization.

Prevention of pollution—Use of processes, practices, materials, or products that avoid, reduce, or control pollution, which may include recycling, treatment, process changes, control mechanisms, efficient use of resources, and material substitution.

Index